CONTENTS

For my grandson
Edmund Ralph Workman

EDUCATION MATTERS

General Editor: Ted Wragg

GROWTH IN CHILDREN

GROWTH IN CHILDREN

John Brierley

With a preface by Professor
James Tanner, FRCP

CASSELL

Cassell Educational Limited

Villiers House
41/47 Strand
London WC2N 5JE, England

387 Park Avenue South
New York
NY 10016–8810, USA

First published 1992

British Library Cataloguing-in-Publication Data
A catalogue record for this book is available from the British Library.

Library of Congress Cataloging-in-Publication Data
Available from the Library of Congress.

ISBN 0–304–32601–1 (hardback)
0–304–32581–3 (paperback)

Phototypeset by Intype, London
Printed and bound in Great Britain by
Biddles Ltd, Guildford and King's Lynn

FOREWORD

Professor E. C. Wragg, Exeter University

During the 1980s a succession of Education Acts changed considerably the nature of schools and their relationships with the outside world. Parents were given more rights and responsibilities, including the opportunity to serve on the governing body of their child's school. The 1988 Education Reform Act in particular, by introducing for the first time a National Curriculum, the testing of children at the ages of 7, 11, 14 and 16, local management, including financial responsibility, and the creation of new types of school, was a radical break with the past. Furthermore the disappearance of millions of jobs, along with other changes in our society, led to reforms not only of schools, but also of further and higher education.

In the wake of such rapid and substantial changes it was not just parents and lay people, but also teachers and other professionals working in education, who found themselves struggling to keep up with what these many changes meant and how to get the best out of them. The *Education Matters* series addresses directly the major topics of reform, such as the new curriculum, testing and assessment, the role of parents and the handling of school finances, considering their effects on primary, secondary, further and higher education, and also the continuing education of adults.

The aim of the series is to present information about the challenges facing education in the remainder of the twentieth century in an authoritative but readable form. The books in the series, therefore, are of particular interest to parents, governors and all those concerned with education, but are written in such a way as to give an overview to students, experienced teachers and other professionals who work in the field.

Each book gives an account of the relevant legislation and background, but, more importantly, stresses practical implications of change with specific examples of what is being or can be done to make reforms work effectively. The authors are not only authorities in their field, but also have direct experience of the matters they write about. That is why the *Education Matters* series makes an important contribution to both debate and practice.

ACKNOWLEDGEMENTS

This book is based on many talks given at science, health education and child development courses during my 25 years' service as HMI and also on the experience of the many class teachers in primary and secondary schools I had the privilege of visiting.

Although the picture is changing, insufficient weight is still given in training courses or in schools to a knowledge and understanding of children's growth and development and to the conditions which affect them. I have not attempted to discuss teaching strategies but two general points emerge, especially in relation to health education. First, the importance of a variety of approach and method in teaching about such subjects as diet and smoking; this is because individuals vary and different approaches will have different impacts on individuals. Second, the futility of strident campaigns about healthy diets, etc., which lead to many adolescents taking the opposite line.

In writing this book I am especially indebted to Emeritus Professor James Tanner, FRCP, whom I first met over 30 years ago when he contributed to a Ministry course on primary education. He brought to us then not only crucial facts about human growth and development which most of us did not know, but also new perspectives, setting them in an educational context. What a pity it is, I thought, that ministers and other policy-makers could not hear him and take note of his words. For me, now, he has not only read this book and improved it but has also written the Preface. For all these services now and long ago I wish to thank him.

My wife, Dr A. F. Brierley, has also read the book and made beneficial comments.

I am indebted to Mr A. J. Rose, HM Chief Inspector DES, for help with references; to Dr Diana Ernaelsteen, Senior Medical Officer at the Department of Health, for advice; and to Mr Alan Edwards for supplying photographs.

Mrs Martina Anderson has, with great care and patience, typed the book from my manuscript drafts.

Any errors of fact and judgement that remain are my own.

John Brierley
Formerly HM Staff Inspector, DES
1992

PREFACE

'At the heart of the educational process lies the child.' So runs the first sentence of the Plowden Report on Primary Education (1966). It continues: 'No advances in policy, no acquisitions of new equipment have the desired effects unless they are in harmony with the nature of the child ... knowledge of the manner in which children develop, therefore, is of prime importance, both in avoiding harmful practices and introducing effective ones.'

The passage of 25 years has in no way diminished these truths; on the contrary, research, often basic and sometimes on species other than our own, has made the details on which these generalisations rest clearer. This is particularly so in two areas: the importance of critical or 'sensitive' periods in the growth and development of the brain, and the importance of the social milieu of the first two or three years of the child's life in relation to ultimate growth, ability, health, and length of life.

These are matters, then, of overwhelming importance to parents, schoolteachers of all age levels, health educators, and politicians concerned with the quality of the nation and the idea of social justice. Yet the truth, I fear, is that in all these groups knowledge of children's development and concern for its importance has positively declined since the optimistic days of Plowden.

John Brierley's book seeks to reverse this decline; to point out to teachers that 'readiness to read' (for example) is more than an empty phrase, that biological variability in tempo of growth is more than an auxological curiosity, that the continuing social class difference in children's growth, no longer present in such countries as Norway and Sweden, is more than a clubroom joke. The growth of children, it has been said, is a 'mirror of the condition of society'. This book helps us hold up that mirror; and if what we see makes us a little ashamed – either of our ignorance or of our complacency – then it would

indeed be a fitting culmination of John Brierley's long years
as HMI.

J. M. Tanner
Institute of Child Health
London University

'After the family the teacher is the most important influence on the next generation.'

Houghton Report on the Pay of Non-university Teachers, 1974.

'Fancy living in one of these streets, never seeing anything beautiful, never eating anything savoury – never saying anything clever.'

Winston Churchill to his private secretary, Edward March, on visiting the slums of Manchester during the 1905 election campaign

INTRODUCTION

This book is about growth, from conception to the end of puberty. During this period there are especially sensitive times when growth – physical, intellectual and emotional – is particularly influenced by environmental factors. Growth can be measured in a variety of ways but perhaps growth in height tells us the most about the health and development of children. Smallness in itself is not a bad thing, but if it results from the potential for height being unfulfilled there is some cause for concern.

I have chosen five periods for detailed consideration of growth, dietary needs, implications for health, and for education where appropriate.

1 Pregnancy.
2 The first year of life.
3 The nursery school years, 2–5.
4 Primary school, 5–11.
5 Puberty.

This choice is based on a single principle. Each period contains times when the brain and nervous system are especially sensitive to the effects of the environment. These sensitive or 'critical' periods are time-limited and if wasted through neglect or by adverse circumstances their usefulness is lost. Only the sketchiest idea of the timing and duration of these periods exists for ourselves but there are rough pointers. When growth varies in pace, being sometimes faster, sometimes slower, as it does between conception and the end of puberty, it is likely that there will be a critical time or times within it. On the other hand, when the body stops growing and simply ticks over, maintaining life processes, no critical periods exist. So, for example, the relatively fast growth of the foetus makes it particularly sensitive to the quality of nutrition and to smoking, drugs and infection. The first year of life emerges as crucial to later physical, emotional and mental health and at this time the rate of growth is fast, though falling. The nursery school years are highly critical. During this time the brain and sense organs are growing fast, the rest of the body quite fast, and stimulus at home and school is essential. The statutory school years (5–16) have multiple critical times in them. During this span, growth rate is steady but there is in most children a mid-childhood spurt from about 6 to 8, plus the rapid spurt of growth at puberty. The whole period requires good schooling – not as a luxury but as a necessity. It also requires at home and school the maintenance of confidence and self-worth. Both are fragile and are easily diminished.

There is no magic age when a once-and-for-all boost of extra resources will have a lasting effect. Each and every age requires the best possible environment; each will influence the next so that the final structure can rest on sound foundations. What a waste of these pre-set times for the two million children who get a raw deal at school.[1] If they do, the resolve of parents and children to persist in education and to have high expectations is weakened and the cycle of neglect and waste is perpetuated. Adverse family circumstances will also impede growth and development and may lead to physical ill-health in later life. When both home and school fail, the result is a disaster. That is why school is of such profound importance to tens of thousands of children from bad homes.

Heredity cannot be neglected, of course, and will interact with a multitude of environmental influences to produce an enormous range of talents and abilities. It also sets a limit to what can be achieved in the best circumstances.

Negative factors which will impede the development of physical, emotional and intellectual potential are: malnutrition before and after birth; smoking and drinking in pregnancy, and probably afterwards though less directly; prolonged illness in the mother before and after birth; lack of opportunities for exploration, play and talk at home; no opportunity for nursery education; poor schooling; lack of sleep; noise; anxiety; pollution of the environment by lead. In short, an adverse family life and poor schools.

Positive factors which will develop physical, emotional and intellectual potential are: interaction with a good environment, including the chance to express ideas and feelings readily; good models to observe at home and school; the development early on of self-reliance and belief in oneself; success for each and every child, however small. In short, a secure family life and good schools.

In many developing countries of the world the solution to much ill-health and backwardness is to provide clean water and sufficient food, and teach the young to read. In this country these are taken for granted and improvement to the system already in operation is needed in five areas to provide:

1 Nursery schools and classes at age 3 for all who want them. At present only 20 per cent of under-5s receive nursery education, which is the best provision for this age group.[2]
2 Better-quality schooling in the statutory school years. The recent HMI report[1] on standards in education does not augur well for the one-third of school children subjected to poor teaching.
3 Better health education in schools which would stress that much of our health lies in our own hands.
4 A strengthened health visitor service. The work of this service is a blessing to the majority of young mothers and is a fount of information and support, and a ready help in trouble.
5 Access to higher education and employment earned by ability and character, not wealth or family connections.

Utopian solutions are useless, but the time is ripe to divert money from military expenditure to education and health. Idealism is a good driving force:

> Come my friends,
> 'Tis not too late to seek a newer world.[3]

References

1 DES, *Standards in Education, 1988–89* (HMSO, 1990).
2 DES, *The Education of Children under Five* (HMSO, 1989).
3 'Ulysses', Alfred, Lord Tennyson.

Chapter 1

GROWTH: A YARDSTICK OF HEALTH AND WELL-BEING

Growth in height is a characteristic of childhood which adults have lost. It is also an index to the kind of life a child leads. Growth in height is not just a mechanical matter of good food and money, it is, as J. M. Tanner wrote, 'a mirror of conditions in society'.[1] The number of children in a family, whether the father is in regular work, whether the child has free meals or not at school, whether the home is a happy one, whether the parents smoke, whether the mother has looked after herself and the baby before it was born and afterwards – all these many influences touch on growth. Indeed, height provides a kind of scale for solid assessments of these many facets of life. Weight is also valuable as a growth measure but it has a smaller value than height because it is sensitive to trivial changes in nutrition or to acute or minor illness. It can also be lost as well as gained. Used together, height and weight provide the best combination for monitoring health and general development.

None of this is to say that small stature is bad. If the inherited potential is for small ultimate stature, smallness is fine; but there is a complex relationship between the influence of environmental circumstances, genetic inheritance and varying levels of height. Small stature may arise because of poor growth of the foetus in pregnancy and early life due to malnutrition (see Chapter 2).

Techniques for measuring height and weight are not the subject of this book and are described by experts elsewhere.[2] Briefly, growth in height or weight is recorded on 'centile' charts. The printed lines on the chart (see Figure 1.1) show roughly the kind of growth expected and the middle heavy line represents the national average or 'standard'. This is called the 50th centile, meaning that the height or weight of 50 per cent

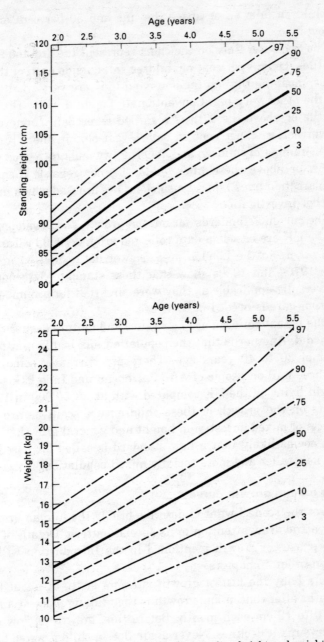

Figure 1.1 Centile charts of 'standards' for standing height and weight for boys aged 2 to 5 years (see text for explanation). Adapted from *Foetus into Man* by J. M. Tanner (Castlemead, 1989).

of children falls on or above the line and 50 per cent on or below it.

The two outer lines on the chart represent the 3rd and 97th centiles. Only 3 per cent of children fall outside each of these lines, meaning that on the one hand they are very small and on the other very big. Conventionally, a child below the 3rd centile or above the 97th is regarded as probably abnormal. Nevertheless, 3 per cent of, say, 8-year-olds in the UK is a large number of children and abnormality must lie a good way below or above these lines. J. M. Tanner regards them as 'demarcation lines' where 'suspicions' are aroused which merit further investigation.

The current 'standards' for normal growth and development in the UK are based on data collected around 1960 by Tanner and others in the London area. Newer data collected in the late 1970s and 1980s show that these standards are not as universally applicable as they were, and that for a number of reasons care is needed in their use.

One is that children are now taller and mature earlier than they did. Another is that the population mix is different from that of 30 to 40 years ago. There are currently some two to three million people of Afro-Caribbean and Indo-Pakistani origin living in the UK compared with about 50,000 in 1951. Facts on the growth of these children are scant as are the effects of mixed ancestry on height and general growth.

It seems likely that a new standard is called for based on the new taller and more racially mixed population.[3]

The human growth curve

To set the scene I want to describe briefly the human growth curve and draw attention to its special pattern. Details of the five phases of growth mentioned in the Introduction will be given in later chapters.

In a baby the fastest growth is *before* birth, at about four months after conception; growth is then taking place at a rate of 10 to 12 cm each month. Before this, growth is slow and afterwards it declines. Never again does a child grow so fast.

Growth after birth

Growth in height is an increase in the distance from the top of the head to the heels. The speed or 'velocity' of this growth is the increase in distance over a certain period of time, mainly measured in centimetres per year. Velocity or rate is used in exactly the same way as when talking about the speed of cars in miles per hour. Just as a car may speed up or slow down within an hour, so the speed of growth may change from one part of a year to another. However, this is not to say that growth takes place in fits and starts – it is a smooth process.

The way growth proceeds in a boy is shown in the two graphs of growth in Figure 1.2. In the top graph (a), his height at each stage is plotted, with the bottom one (b) showing his rate or velocity of growth. Interestingly, the record is the oldest published study of the growth of a child and was made about 200 years ago. The velocity curve is especially illuminating because it shows that the speed of growth is not constant and emphasises the possible stages of critical times. At birth a child is growing faster than at any other time in life but not as fast as before birth. But the speed of growth in height declines from birth onwards. It is in early childhood that the drop in speed of growth is most dramatic. It then declines very slowly, and from about the age of 6 until puberty is reached growth in height is nearly constant year by year – though not quite. There is a slight increase in velocity between 6 and 8 in many children and this is called the 'mid-growth' spurt. It can be seen on the graph. Then quite suddenly during the adolescent spurt, the slow rate is reversed and there is a dramatic acceleration. For a year or two the child shoots up, growing at the same rate as when he was 2 or 3. After this burst, the speed of growth declines, becomes progressively slower, and stops – usually at about 17½ in boys and 15½ in girls in Western Europe.

This description is a coarse one and there are finer periods of growth which underline the general growth rate. Within a year's space, as parents must have noticed, children of between 5 and 9 do not grow at the same rate. For some the slowest growth takes place during autumn and winter, the fastest between January and July.[4] For others there are comparable

7

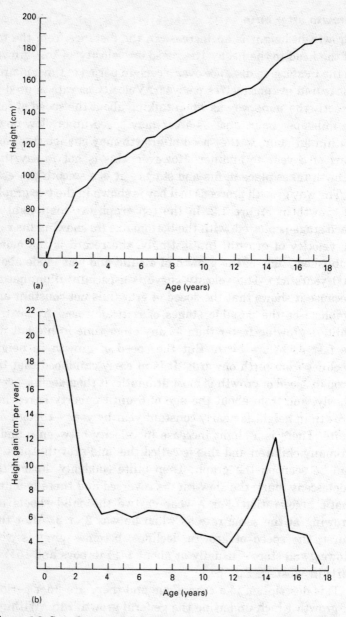

Figure 1.2 Growth in height of Count de Montbeillard's son from birth to age 18 (1759–77). (a) shows the 'distance' curve: height attained at each age in centimetres; (b) the 'velocity' curve showing increments in height gained from year to year. From *Education and Physical Growth* by J. M. Tanner (University of London Press, 1961).

changes in growth rate, apparently independent of season. Before about 5, when the speed of growth is decelerating rapidly, and during the adolescent spurt, seasonal changes in growth rate are masked by the speed of the overall change. Growth in weight is fastest in the autumn.

There is some slight evidence that day length, which varies during the seasons and which is perceived through the eyes, may affect growth, perhaps by influencing the glands in the brain that control growth. In totally blind children the rate of growth does not vary much with the seasons in the way that it does with children of normal sight. This is not to say that blind children grow at a constant rate but that their fastest and slowest growth may take place in any season.

Growth as described in Figure 1.2 is perfectly true for the normal child, but there are wide variations between individuals of the same sex and considerable differences between boys and girls. These differences can be troublesome to the persons themselves, to parents and to teachers. At the top of the primary school some of the girls will be physically well-developed and will be menstruating but the boys remain little boys. This is because puberty begins on average about two years earlier in girls, with a peak growth rate at age 12. For boys this comes on average at about 14.

Tall and short[5, 6]

In both boys and girls great variations in growth pattern exist and there are extremes of tallness and shortness above the 97th or below the 3rd centile.

A boy or girl who is very tall compared with friends, or with parents who themselves are very tall and who are worried because they think they may have an exceptionally tall child, sometimes seeks medical advice. Most of the children are fortunately perfectly normal and well, but girls may still be worried for social reasons.

Predictions of future height, which has a high inherited component, can be made from the child's own height at age 2 until the start of puberty. Tables are necessary to do this but even so the error is quite considerable – within 15 cm. Much more often than treatment, reassurance is necessary from doctors, teachers and parents that a tall child will not end up a giant. Tall girls especially tend to slouch and need to be encouraged to hold themselves straight. If a specialist decides that her tallness is not due to a medical condition it may be necessary to decide on purely social grounds whether a girl's final height prediction is acceptable or not. If it is not, a doctor might prescribe large daily doses of oestrogen hormone to stop the growth spurt sooner than it would if left to itself. But the risks of hormone treatment are considerable and such treatment needs to be very selective. Alternatively, but rarely, a tall girl can have her legs shortened by bone surgery in later life.

Sometimes a child is tiny and parents are anxious to find out whether his or her growth is normal or not. Perhaps the parents are tall, or the boy or girl is the smallest in the class, or a younger child in the family is bigger, or he or she is not growing out of clothes like other children. A doctor should always be seen if the child fails to gain height so that proper treatment can be obtained if necessary.

Apart from some abnormalities, growth rates can be hampered by bad feeding, smoking in pregnancy (and afterwards by parents' smoking), disease and unhappiness. Return to normal height is accompanied by a big catch-up growth to a normal pattern. How this catch-up growth is regulated is not understood but its machinery is so sensitive and effective that it allows growth to return almost completely to its previous pattern after a set-back.

The special pattern of human growth

The special pattern of human growth is graphically displayed in Richard Scammon's[7] famous diagram of the four types of growth (see Figure 1.3). Notice how fast the brain, head and sense organs develop in marked contrast to the slower growth of the body as a whole and of the reproductive organs. The lymphatic system grows to almost twice adult size by the time a child is about 10 and then shrinks to adult proportions by about 20. Its swift development is a defence against infection, and the baby and infant freshly exposed to the world rapidly

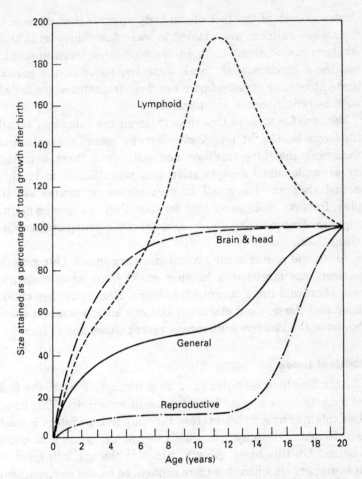

Figure 1.3 Growth graphs of different parts of the body. The graphs show size achieved and are given as a percentage of total gain from birth to 20 years so that size at 20 is 100 per cent. From *An Introduction to the Study of Man* by J. Z. Young (Oxford University Press, 1971).

develop immunity. The reproductive organs develop late because early in life a child is not ready to reproduce.

There are two major points: first, the 'long childhood' sandwiched between birth and puberty is a time when the brain, head and sense organs are growing fast and learning potential is at flood readiness; second, general growth and maturity are delayed until puberty.

The paradox between the rapid growth of the head and the

11

slower growth of the rest of the body ensures that there is a time when children are adapted to learn fast. Early on in this whole period of about 12 to 14 years children learn to speak, use their hands and to think logically. Later in the period these attributes develop further and other qualities are added such as reflectiveness and idealism.

Because for most of this time children are relatively small they can be taught and 'controlled' by elders (parents and teachers), absorbing tradition and skills from them, learning by example and by exploration and play. Early on in this period they are too small to hurt others or themselves in play. Puberty changes all this, for then they too become adult, capable of reproducing and looking after the young and dominating them.

All this of course is the evolutionary argument. Our growth pattern was forged in a harsher world than now, when life was short and there was much to learn. Hence the long childhood and the delayed maturity. Old age and its wisdom are a bonus of the relative affluence of recent times and of luck.

Critical times

Within this long sensitive time from conception up to the end of puberty there appear to be degrees of sensitivity. This must be explained by a biological law: that any living system is most sensitive and modified most easily during periods of maximum change. On this basis, growth, which is change, will have in it some periods when it is more influenced by the environment than it is at other times simply because growth is sometimes relatively fast, sometimes slow. Maintenance processes, where the body ticks over ensuring that life processes go on, proceed at fairly uniform rates and should not manifest critical periods.

Developmental processes, like growth, vary in rate and duration in three basic ways:[8]

1 Growth and development may proceed rapidly for a short time and then stop.
2 They may proceed rapidly, falling off afterwards to a low level but never quite stopping.
3 They may be rapid but intermittent.

These three patterns link with the growth curves in Figures 1.2 and 1.3 and have different implications for critical periods.

The timing and duration of critical times in ourselves are vaguer than in some other animals. A bird rapidly learns to sing and fly at an appropriate stage but progress is slow once the short crucial stage has passed. More precisely, on timing, if a kitten is deprived of a certain stimulus (a pattern) between the fourth and seventh weeks after birth, the cells of the visual cortex of the brain do not respond to the stimulus by the discharge of an electrical signal. Deprivation of the pattern for as little as three to four days when the critical time is at its peak, in the third and fourth week after birth, leads to a sharp reduction in the number of responding cells and the pattern is clearly not perceived.

Some stages of human development show the short, sharp, critical period (1 above), particularly in the development of the embryo. Certain drugs (e.g. thalidomide) adversely affect the development of limbs in the first twelve weeks but not after. Some children whose mothers catch German measles between the first and twelfth weeks of pregnancy are born with eye and other defects. After the twelfth week infection has no effect.

Behaviour and learning have parallels with patterns (2) and (3) above.[8] Pattern (2), when growth proceeds rapidly before falling off to a lower level (though not ceasing until after puberty), is characteristic of the social attachment process in animals. Attachments can be made within a few minutes in chicks, as little as two hours in dogs and about ten days in lambs. A baby's most rapid attachment period occurs from approximately five to six weeks to six to seven months from birth. (Babies adopted *before* six months show fewer psychological problems later compared with those adopted later.) Attachment in ourselves is complex and is explained further in Chapter 5, but it continues to be strengthened throughout the nursery years and to a lesser degree of intensity in the primary school years.

Pattern 2 has parallels with the human growth rate curve (see Figure 1.2b). In the first year of life bonding is strong when growth rate is fast, marking a highly critical time; it then continues through the nursery and primary years when growth rate is falling and attachment behaviour is less strong, though continually reinforced. The puberty spurt loosens ties and breaks them in some so that at 16 or 17 the child becomes an adult free or freer of home ties.

Critical times and school

Learning goes on throughout life, but the rapid growth rate of the brain and sense organs up to about 8 (see Figure 1.3) highlights a highly critical time for learning. At this time mental development is fast, with about 80 per cent of IQ being achieved by the age of 8. The general growth-rate curve shown in Figure 1.2b is also instructive and fits into pattern (3) above. In this, growth proceeds intermittently at high rates and shows multiple critical periods. Figure 1.2b shows growth from birth to puberty as relatively fast, and though dropping in rate it can be seen that this fall is broken by a small spurt from about 6 to 8 and a big spurt at puberty.

The whole of the time from birth to the end of puberty appears to be a period of high sensitivity rather like a high plateau which is spiked with peaks marking particular sensitive times for learning.[8]

As to the practical significance of these periods for teaching and learning it is important to remember that 'pre-school' education does not begin at 2 or 3 at nursery school or play group but at *birth*, for a child's brain is in action rapidly and learning begins within days of being born. Talk and other stimuli are vital in order to use this critical time well and to lay sound foundations for future progress. No infant teacher needs reminding of the enormous progress made by children between 5 and 7 or 8 – progress which is little short of a miracle. Nor does the junior teacher of 10-year-olds, who at their best can calculate, talk, read and write fluently and consult books like adults. By that age they can have a practised intelligence, disciplined imagination, and a full memory. At puberty all this and more is present, but deepened by reflectiveness and idealism and a capacity to see and understand connections between one thing and another.

These important principles are taken up again in detail in

various chapters but if critical times are neglected by an adverse home and school what might have been learned easily at the right time will be more slowly acquired or not at all. It is not so much a bad start that harms, because the child has natural self-righting tendencies, but a train of disadvantage: poor home and school followed by another poor school.

On this point Horace Barlow wrote recently:

> If mental and moral development in humans follows the crude animal models we have so far, the fear that we do not provide enough intellectual stimulus to the developing mind has more justification than the fear that it will be warped by unsuitable experience.[9]

Brain connectivity

In ourselves the nature of the physical base of these critical times is speculative but must be lodged in the brain cells. It is likely that there are times (the critical periods) when nerve cells in widespread areas of the brain can perpetually alter their connections in response to environmental influences. Some nerve pathways may remain plastic for a very short time during which their 'wiring' is finely tuned. Disruption by drugs or infection during pregnancy may sharply distort the wiring pattern and lead to the defects described earlier. Other pathways may have an ongoing ability for longer or shorter periods to alter their wiring, a capacity which is important to teaching and learning.

With regard to teaching and learning animal experiments show that if the perception of a stimulus is blocked[10] (or the stimulus is low), developing nerve cells may freeze in an immature state or have their development distorted: that is, they may fail to branch out to form a rich network of nerve connections with the result that alterations of behaviour occur. Learning involves assembling and strengthening some nerve connections and abolishing others. A poor home and school life may well affect human nerve patterns in this way, but at present such knowledge is beyond the microscope.

How a critical time is started and stopped is not understood but genes that act as 'on/off' switches must be involved. At present, however, as explained in this chapter, only the measures of overall growth rates of the body and its parts such as the head give us a clue to the timing and extent of these periods in ourselves. Although overall growth ceases, nerve cells in *certain* parts of the brain may be able to change and respond to stimuli so that new skills can be picked up in middle and old age, though more slowly; but skills such as writing and our way of speaking – both established early – remain as fresh as when first laid down (see Chapter 7). Witness the persisting constancy of our handwriting and our dialect over a span of 50 years.

References

1 J. M. Tanner, 'Growth as a mirror of the conditions of society: secular trends and class distinctions', in A. Demirijian (ed.), *Human Growth: A Multidisciplinary Review* (Taylor & Francis, 1986).

2 J. M. Tanner, *Foetus into Man* (Castlemead, 1989).

3 R. J. Rona and S. Chinn, 'National study of health and growth. . .', *Annals of Human Biology* **13** (1986).

4 W. A. Marshall, 'Growth in children: understanding growth rates', *Update* **3** (1971).

5 W. A. Marshall, 'Growth in children: the tall child', *Update* **3** (1972).

6 W. A. Marshall, 'Growth in children: is he too small?', *Update* **3** (1972).

7 In J. Z. Young, *An Introduction to the Study of Man* (Oxford University Press, 1971).

8 J. P. Scott, 'Critical periods in organisational processes', in F. Falkner and J. M. Tanner (eds), *Human Growth* (Plenum Press, 1986).

9 Horace Barlow, Preface to John Brierley, *Give Me a Child Until He Is Seven* (Falmer Press, 1987).

10 R. E. Kalil, 'Synapse formation in the developing brain', *Scientific American* (December 1989).

Chapter 2

HEREDITY AND GROWTH

Parents are quick to notice differences between their children, height being a common talking point – and among girls, size of feet which achieve adult size early! Teachers are also well aware of the variations in growth and development of their charges. One head of a Nottingham inner-city primary school once asked me how old I thought a class of children were. I was out by a year. The relative smallness of inner-city children had misled me.

Height, like most human characteristics, is a product of the interaction of heredity and environmental influences. With regard to heredity, we have been formed by a kind of genetic lottery and each one of us is but one of a vast number of possible children any of whom might have been conceived and born if a different sperm or egg, each carrying its own set of genes, had fused.

Each fertilised egg has a unique set of potentialities determined by the genetic code carried on the chromosomes. Whether these potentialities will develop and how they will do so depends on the environment. These environmental influences are probably countless and powerful, and some are difficult to quantify. Many are unidentifiable.

Birth weight, for example, is subject to a complex of influences. L. S. Penrose attempted to unravel the causes of variation in the weight of babies at birth.[1] He estimated that about 38 per cent of the variation was due to inherited factors such as the sex and the hereditary constitution of the mother and child. Environmental factors such as maternal health and nutrition, and the mother's age, contributed about 32 per cent to the variation. It is not surprising that 30 per cent of the causes of weight variation remain unknown. Indeed, it would be remarkable if all the differences between human beings could be pinned down and accounted for but it is important that we should understand more of the reasons behind the differences, especially of behaviour, if we are to conduct our affairs better.

In the UK, height variation is largely due to inherited factors because children usually get enough to eat and are seldom stunted by preventable disease. In poorer parts of the world, where food is short and doctors scarce, a greater proportion of height variation is due to environmental causes.

Ethnic minority and inner-city children

Despite the vast amount of evidence amassed about the growth and development of children there are still surprisingly big gaps in the understanding of height and of the relative importance of heredity and environment. For example, in England in 1983 children of ethnic minorities in the primary age range were, with the exception of the Afro-Caribbean group, shorter than the 'standard', that is, the representative of the English population. So too were children who lived in inner cities. The Afro-Caribbean children were 3–4 cm taller, Gujarati children about 3 cm smaller, and English inner-city children about 1 cm shorter than the standard height.

The difficulties of applying currently used standards for height, based on a predominantly 'English' sample of children, to ethnic minorities have been mentioned, but these large variations between different ethnic groups are complex. For example, in the English group of children, the number of siblings in the family, type of school meal and father's employment status are strongly linked with a child's height (see Table 2.1). For the Asian group of children, overcrowding in the home and the mother's education seem more important. For the Afro-Caribbean children most social factors are significantly related to a child's height. Even though many social matters seem to be associated with height, they explain only a small proportion of the variation in children's height; their genes are likely to explain more.

One broad 'social' conclusion is that where the mother works full-time outside the home, children are better fed and taller. Table 2.1 is particularly instructive about the strong link between stature and free meals.

18

Table 2.1 Factors influencing the heights of schoolchildren

	Age 10–11 years		Age 14–15 years	
	Boys	*Girls*	*Boys*	*Girls*
Father in non-manual occupation (compared with manual)	Taller**	No trend perceived	Taller*	Taller*
Father employed (compared with unemployed)	Taller**	Taller**	Taller*	Taller*
Child from a family receiving supplementary benefit (compared with a family not receiving)	Shorter**	Shorter**	Shorter**	Shorter**
Child receiving free school meals (compared with those not receiving)	Shorter**	Shorter**	Shorter**	Shorter**
Percentage of children receiving free school meals	19	21	15	12
British Standard (cm: 50th centile)[5]	139.3	139.5	164.0	161.1
Total sample: 1983 (cm: mean heights)	142.8	142.9	166.8	161.0

** Statistically significant trend.
* Trend apparent but it does not achieve statistical significance.
Source: Adapted from *On the State of the Public Health for the Year 1988* (HMSO, 1989).

Type of school meal – whether free, purchased or made at home – is related to height, and children who have free meals are consistently shorter than those who do not. Indeed, free meals are a good general index of the effect of a number of social factors which affect height (see Table 2.1).

Polygenes and height

These examples and those of birth weight underline the non-sense of such blanket statements as 'height is 80 per cent

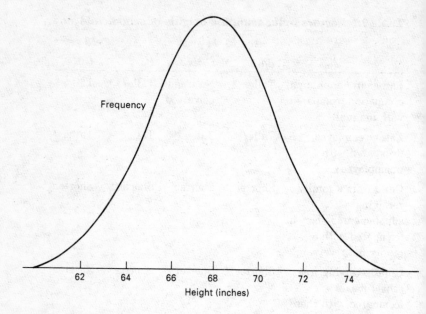

Figure 2.1 A distribution curve for height in full-grown men in south-east England. Adapted from *Human Heredity* by C. O. Carter (Pelican Books, 1963).

heredity and 20 per cent environment'. Heredity and environment interact in the production of most characteristics – height, intelligence, birth weight – and it cannot be said what proportion has been contributed by each.

Some inherited characteristics are clear cut, like blue or brown eyes or the blood groups, but most human differences are by no means sharply distinguished, height and 'intelligence' among them. These vaguer characteristics are called 'continuous' because they run into each other. A marriage between a tall man and a small woman does not produce clear-cut families of tall and short children, because height is controlled by many genes producing small additive effects. Neither will a sample of 1,000 men fall into two or three sharply defined heights: they will vary in stature over a fairly limited range and within this range very tall and very short men are uncommon. This effect is shown in Figure 2.1.

Francis Galton found the clue to the explanation of these

rather indefinite kinds of variations. He thought that finely graded characteristics like height or intelligence were controlled by a mosaic of small, inherited units. It has been shown, largely as a result of breeding work with small fruit flies called *Drosophila*, that these polygenes as they are called, are, like the obvious 'major' genes (which control blood groups for example), situated on the chromosomes but instead of producing a sharp, clear-cut effect, they work in groups. Each member of a group has a small quantitative effect, plus or minus, on a major characteristic like height. The smooth curve for height shown is due, of course, not only to the work of polygenes affecting limb length and head and body sizes independently but also to the effects of the environment.

The secular trend

Estimates of the interplay of the polygenes and environmental influences are given rather strikingly by the analysis of the trend in children's growth and development over the last 150 years. Technically this is called the secular trend, a curious expression meaning something that proceeds slowly yet persistently. In this case it means the tendency of children to get larger and to mature earlier, tendencies that are usually linked. Interestingly, the trend in height has the maximum effect *between ages 9 and 12*.[3]

If we look back to the 1830s, we see that children were much smaller than now. A graph of heights of factory girls is shown in Figure 2.2. Then, a girl of 12 was about 20 cm shorter than the current average and a girl of 8 about 12 cm shorter. An 8-year-old was about 7 kg and a 12-year-old 15 kg lighter than now. A similar story can be told for boys.

The children were tiny and it is easy to imagine them at, say, 5 and 6 crawling under machines picking up cotton waste or, when a bit older, being sent up chimneys.

Exact measurements of height and weight are available from these past times, not for any scientific reason but because they were used as a check to stop the falsification of children's ages by parents who wanted to collect the wages for adult hours of work obtainable at 13.[3]

The trend in the UK, starting from around 1900, was still

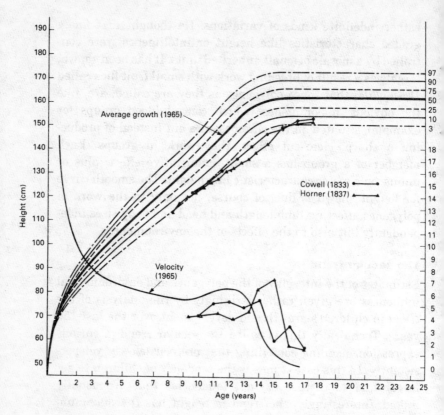

Figure 2.2 Standard heights of girls (1965) compared with mean heights of girls working in factories in the Manchester–Leeds areas in 1833 and 1837. Means for 1833 have been adjusted by subtraction of 0.5 cm for footwear. The continuous lower graph represents the 1965 average velocity of growth. Note the later growth spurt of the factory girls, especially in Cowell's data. From *A History of the Study of Human Growth* by J. M. Tanner (Cambridge University Press, 1981).

going throughout the 1970s at about 0.8 cm and 0.5 cm/decade for boys and girls respectively,[4] but it has now slowed or even stopped in the UK and in many European countries as the limit set by the genes is reached (though curiously it persists in such well-off countries as Holland and Switzerland).

What are the reasons for the trend and why did it start? They are not fully understood but it is likely that the acceleration of growth was due to rising standards of nutrition and quality of environment. A reduction in disease must also have contributed. Probably the genetic limits for height have now been reached for most children in the UK.

Age of menarche

There has been a similar trend in the attainment of maturity in both boys and girls, so that in the UK, for example, the age of menarche (the first menstrual period) has been getting earlier by about four months/decade over the whole period from 1880 to 1960. There is still wide variation in the time at which menarche occurs, but in 1830 the average age was 15.2 (range 11–20).[3] It now begins on average at 13 with a range of 9.5–14.5. This trend is happening, like the increase in height, all over the world. Obviously it will stop somewhere, and it may have done so by now in the UK as the limits set by heredity are reached.

Twins and triplets

Perhaps the least elusive illustration of the interplay of heredity and environment on growth and development is provided by studies of twins and triplets.

About one in 88 maternities produces twins. Sometimes these develop from one fertilised egg which splits into two embryos to form twins. In 90 per cent of cases these 'one-egg' twins are identical; two duplicate human beings with the same packet of genes, nature, character and sex. There is another, commoner type of twin which results from two separately fertilised eggs; the twins need not be of the same sex and need be no more alike than ordinary brothers and sisters. This is because on average they have only half their chromosomes in common. The two kinds of twins, identical or one-egg and fraternal or two-egg, occur in the ratio of about 1:2.5. The chance of producing identical twins is about one in 300 births. Triplets, quadruplets and quintuplets are varieties of, or combinations of, one-egg and two-egg twins and have been called 'super-twins'. Siamese twins arise from *one* fertilised egg that splits late into two separate embryos which are joined together in any one of a variety of ways.

How can the comparison of twins be used to estimate the

relative importance of nature and nurture in growth, for example? One-egg twins, since they have a common hereditary endowment, can be used to estimate the differences which arise entirely from environment. Even in the uterus their different positions put them in slightly different environments from the outset. More striking, one-egg twins may be brought up apart, as sometimes happens when they are orphaned and separated at birth, and so comparisons about the effects of the environment on a common heredity can be made.

Two-egg twins have quite different gene outfits since each egg has been fertilised by a different sperm. They can be used to estimate the strength of genetic differences since the family environment is common for both of them.

I have deliberately used the word 'estimate' in describing twin studies and the effects of heredity and environment, simply because twins do not give us the clear-cut separation that the early studies hoped for. One-egg twins do not always have the same chromosome outfits. One may lose a sex chromosome as the fertilised egg splits, and change its sex. Moreover, if the cytoplasm round the egg splits unevenly one twin may lose a foot, or have a different temperament or intelligence from the other. Two-egg twins are formed from *whole* eggs so there are no cytoplasmic differences. Any differences depend on how widely their chromosomes differ. Sometimes they are very similar with the effect that two-egg twins can be alike in many ways.

Some comparisons of twins have shown that certain characteristics are strongly inherited and are quite unaffected by environment. These are the blood group and fingerprint patterns. Other characteristics are almost as strongly inherited but can be slightly changed by the environment. Some of these are eye and hair colour, shape, length and colour of eyelashes and eyebrows, complexion, presence or absence or size and number of freckles, size and shape of nose, mouth and ears, teeth shape.

With regard to growth, if the growth curves of triplets are examined where two are *identical* twins and the third fraternal, the twins' growth patterns resemble each other much more closely than they resemble that of the fraternal individual. These differences show up in pre-pubertal growth, in final stature, and in the pace or 'tempo' of growth.

These observations, and those from other family studies which include identical and non-identical twins, parent–child and sib–sib correlations, give an overall impression of genetic machinery closely controlling the final height of individuals.

A useful summary in this complex and not well understood territory of growth in children is given by Roberto Rona.[4] He concludes that there is no general rule by which a set proportion of growth is determined by genes and another fixed proportion by environment. Growth of children will depend on the genetic and environmental variability in each country and these are changing over time. The high correlation in most studies between close relatives (e.g., twins and first-degree relatives) is an indication of the influence of genes, but also can be seen as evidence that common family environment may also play a role in the variation of growth.

In the UK, social and health factors such as the father's social class and employment status, number of siblings, and minor respiratory illnesses are significantly associated with height in pre-school children and primary schoolchildren. In the total community in the UK, these factors appear to play a minor role in the variation of height, with the genes playing a more major role. However, in a small proportion of the population, 5 to 10 per cent, many adverse social circumstances are linked and are a threat to the normal growth of children in deprived sectors such as those in inner cities. This matter and that of poverty will be taken up in Chapters 9 and 12.

References

1 L. S. Penrose, *Outline of Human Genetics* (Heinemann, 1963).
2 DHSS, *The Diets of British School Children: A Preliminary Report* (HMSO, 1986).
3 J. M. Tanner, *A History of the Study of Human Growth* (Cambridge University Press, 1981).
4 Roberto Rona, 'Genetic and environmental factors with control of growth in childhood', *British Medical Journal* **37**, no. 3 (1981).

Chapter 3
PREGNANCY 1

It is not surprising that the growth of the baby in pregnancy is relatively ill-understood. Until about ten years ago no direct information was available about the pre-natal growth pattern of a normal baby simply because it is effectively insulated from the outside world. Ultrasonic measurements over the last ten years or so have proved a valuable tool for the study of normal foetal growth and also have provided details on such matters as kidney function and pattern of eye and limb movement. They have also brought to many a young couple the pleasure and fascination of seeing the beauty of their baby at about three months, with its graceful and fluid movements.

Despite these valuable advances, the early stages of pregnancy are still obscure and the embryo is not visible using ultrasonics until about three weeks from conception.[1] These early stages have been studied through direct examination of embryos obtained as a result of hysterectomy or spontaneous abortion. However, many of the latter are abnormal and clearly cannot give much information on normality. Thankfully, the majority of abnormalities seem to be screened out by natural miscarriage during the first three months of pregnancy and only about 30 per cent of conceptions ever survive to birth.

The whole of pregnancy is crucially important to the child's future health and well-being because it is one long critical period. The growth rate of the embryo and foetus as measured in length is not constant but rises to a peak at about 20 weeks from conception and then falls until birth. For the whole of this time the foetus will be sensitive to the effects of drugs, smoking, infection and nutrition.

26

Embryo

The most critical stage, the formation of the spinal cord and brain, is complete by the end of the first two months from conception – the embryonic period – and the eyes and ears are all structurally well-advanced as well. 'Embryo' is from a Greek word meaning to 'teem within', and is a good description because by the end of four weeks the spot of life has grown to about 10,000 times the size of the fertilised egg and by the end of the two months the spot will look like a tiny baby.

The foetal period, which is considered to start at the ninth week from conception, lasts for 30 weeks until birth. 'Fetus' is Latin for 'young one' and is a good description because the embryonic period completes structural organisation while the foetal stage perfects the function of the person.[2]

To be able to write these facts about growth and development in the uterus arrogantly underestimates the fantastic difficulties of the study of tiny, delicate embryos. This smallness has an awesome beauty.

At the end of the embryonic period the embryo is only about 30 mm in length and weighs between 2 and 3 grams. The fertilised egg (seen for the first time less than 50 years ago) is only just visible to the naked eye and is smaller than a full stop. At day five the fertilised egg is a speck about 0.1–0.2 mm in length. The month-old embryo is about 4–6 mm long, half the size of a pea, and has a tail and ridges on the side of the head that look like gill slits. There are buds for arms and legs and primitive eyes and ears. The tail is not a tail but encloses the early spinal cord. The gills are not gills but folds of tissue that provide material for the fashioning of the head and face.[2]

At this time the heart is beating but is just a tube a couple of millimetres long. The month-old embryo is so tiny that the beating heart bulges out, pulsing at 60–70 beats a minute. The head is approximately 2 mm in diameter. It is remarkable that a person's potential is encapsulated in that small space and even more inspiring of wonder to consider that Shakespeare or Beethoven or Constable were so constructed.

At the end of the embryonic period at about eight weeks, the head is more rounded, measuring about 13 mm in diameter and 40 mm in circumference. The limbs are longer and more developed and all four reach about 15 mm in length, the legs exceeding the arms much later. Total length is about 30 mm. The first bone cells are formed in the cartilage skeleton about this time and mark the end of the embryonic stage.

Placenta

Despite the amazing increase in size from the fertilised egg, velocity of growth during the embryonic period is not very great and the rate increases as it enters the foetal stage.

The embryo does not float freely in the uterus. After fertilisation, the fertilised egg drifts down the Fallopian tube, floats for a short time within the uterus, and then implants in the uterus wall. At this stage (fourteen days or so from conception), the embryo has about 130 cells. It is not naked but contained within a membrane – the amnion – surrounded by what is really its own private pond – the amniotic fluid – otherwise the delicate tissues would be dried up and crushed. The fluid-filled chamber in which the embryo and later the foetus develops is commonly called the 'bag of waters' or amniotic sac.

The embryo and foetus depend entirely on the mother for food, at first through minute, finger-like projections that cover the capsule; later, at about the twelfth day from conception, a placenta starts to develop, although it will be several weeks before the familiar disc-shaped structure forms. A full discoid shape can form as early as six weeks. All supplies of food, oxygen and water pass across the placenta to the embryo, and waste substances pass back through from foetus to mother. At first a kind of stalk forms the conducting-channel; this later develops into the umbilical cord.

'Placenta' is Latin for 'cake' and it is indeed cake-shaped. It is rooted in the uterus wall and grows with the developing child up to a weight of between 425 and 550 gm (450 gm = 1 pound); it is about 2–2.5 cm thick when laid flat, but in the uterus it is twice as thick because of its blood content. Its main job is to feed the foetus and bring it oxygen, but it is a versatile and complex structure and nutrients are selectively transferred into the foetal blood.

The placenta grows more rapidly than the foetus but its growth slows markedly after 35 weeks while the foetus continues to grow quite fast. Perhaps the placenta cannot keep pace with foetal growth.

It is important to stress that the three partners in pregnancy – mother, placenta and foetus – interact in a single unit and poor growth of the foetus warns that something is wrong.[3] Those mothers who are living on the poverty line and below it are more likely to have a low-birth-weight baby than other mothers, as the next chapter shows.

Sometimes the placenta becomes disproportionately large (more than 680 gm or 1½ lb). Why this happens is not understood, but only 7 per cent of babies born to mothers in social classes I and II have placentas that weigh more than 1½ lb compared with 24 per cent of those born to mothers in the lower social classes. D. J. P. Barker[4] thinks that poor nutrition is linked with large placental weight, which in turn is associated with adult diseases such as high blood pressure (see Chapter 10).

Foetus

Returning to the foetus: at the beginning of the foetal period it is about 3 cm long. During this stage the various parts of the body differentiate and mature. It is a period of fast growth. The fastest growth happens between the 12th and 36th weeks. In fact, the foetal mass increases 100 times during the last six months of pregnancy. Between 32 and 36 weeks the rate of foetal weight gain reaches its peak at 200–225 gm/week but it declines after this.

The fastest growth in length is at about four months from conception. The high rate of growth of the foetus compared with that of the child is mainly due to the fact that its cells are still dividing, but the proportion of cells undergoing division in any tissue declines as the foetus gets older. Indeed, after about 30 weeks, when growth is declining, few new cells are formed.

Most of the increase in foetal weight up to about six months after conception is due to protein accumulation as the body cells are built up. From then on fat accumulates to provide an energy reserve to be available after birth. The diversion of

29

this energy to the foetus marks a considerable drain on the mother in the last weeks of pregnancy.

Essential activities take place in development and are established before birth in preparation for the needs that arise after birth: the swallowing and sucking reflexes are perfected, sets of muscles to assist breathing are active, and the formation of urine begins.

From about 36 weeks from conception to birth at around 40 weeks the baby slows down in its rate of growth, a process which may be due to the effect of space in the uterus. Twins slow down sooner, when their combined weight is equal to that of a 36-week-old single baby. If the child's hereditary endowment from its parents is for largeness, the slowing-down mechanism helps such a child to be born easily to a small woman. A big child has an inheritance timed to make itself felt only after birth and thus, given the right conditions for growth in the uterus, a baby born small grows fast in the first few years and again in adolescence because of its genetic make-up.

Brain growth in the uterus and up to the age of two

I now want to consider brain growth in the uterus and in early life more specifically and to discuss the influences that may help or hinder its growth and development. Not a great deal is yet known about the brain but enough is understood to take steps that will enhance, rather than baulk, the development of potential, both physical and mental.

The brain grows very fast in the foetus. At about eight weeks from conception it weighs about 2.5 gm; at birth about 380 gm. All the evidence shows that the brain is developing fast. The environment of the baby is disturbed by sounds, light and touch, and it responds by moving. A century ago babies were thought to be born deaf as well as dumb, but it is known now that by mid-pregnancy the baby can hear and respond to a wide variety of sounds, such as the rumbles of the intestines and the sound of the heart. In late pregnancy bright light shone at the uterus can cause movement and change in the electrical activities of the baby's brain. Very early in pregnancy the baby responds to touch.

The big spurt in brain growth starts towards the end of the first six months of pregnancy and ends when the child is about 2 years old.[5] There is a minor spurt earlier which lasts from the twelfth to the eighteenth week of pregnancy. This minor spurt represents the multiplication of nerve cells until adult numbers are achieved. The major spurt already referred to reflects growth and branching of nerve cells with no increase in their number, but both spurts mark a sensitive time for brain development. There is however a massive 'glial' cell multiplication. These glial cells form about 80 per cent of brain weight but what they do is not established. Speculation suggests that they may simply serve as packing material to the neurones, but nature is not so wasteful as this and they are likely to serve some other important purpose such as involvement with memory.

It is pertinent to repeat a general point about critical times and growth at this point: nerve cells are most sensitive to the effects of the environment during times of rapid growth. The brain's two growth spurts are such times. Because of this high sensitivity, if a mother slims before and during pregnancy, takes aspirin, tranquillisers or any other drug, lives by a main road with its fumes and lead dust, regularly enjoys her gin and tonic and smokes cigarettes, the risk of impaired brain growth (and other defects) in her baby increases. If, after the baby is born, a breast-feeding mother does not eat properly, or any mother smokes or neglects her baby the problem compounds. Why is this? The answer is quite simple: because the brain is growing rapidly.

During the major growth spurt, which lasts for 27 or 28 months, important changes take place in the brain cortex, the grey matter of the brain which helps us to think. The billions of nerve cells grow, branch and connect when the child is in the uterus *and* also in the first couple of years of life. The parts of the nerve cells that connect (at nerve synapses) are the fine tendrils called dendrites. Under the microscope a slice of grey matter from a child of 4 looks like a dense forest of branches. At birth there are only a few branches. It is thought, though not established, that the richness of branching and connecting of the dendrites in the grey matter is important in the development of the brain's capabilities, more specifically, 'intelligence'. Only very elementary ways of measuring 'connectivity' are available as yet. Nor is it known, either in children or adults, whether the use made of the brain by thinking and doing influences the branching pattern of the nerve cells. Because of the fast-growing brain it is prudent to provide a good environment for the infant.

Diet

Although energy is needed during pregnancy to support the growth of the foetus and to enable fat to be laid down in the mother's body for use during lactation, considerable reductions occur in physical activity and metabolic rate to help to compensate for the increased needs. A modest increase of about 200 extra calories a day for the final three months is necessary, but women who are underweight at the start of pregnancy may need to eat more.[6]

It is obvious that a mother's diet should contain sufficient energy and protein. But iron, calcium, folic acid and vitamins C and D (and liquid for lactation) are also essential for good growth.[7] If the diet is inadequate, a mother's own store of nutrients will be reduced in order to maintain the foetus. A sound knowledge of nutrition in the mother is invaluable at this time and will help to influence her child's eating habits later.

Critical times

As indicated earlier, the growing embryo and foetus are in a highly sensitive state. Social poisons such as alcohol, cannabis and carbon monoxide from cigarettes which move freely across the placenta are harmful – heavy smoking especially so, as the next chapter shows. Lead from old paint and piping contaminating food and water, as well as lead in petrol, is a poison and may harm mental development, particularly in combination with other adverse influences.

I have given such detailed consideration to pregnancy because during this time a sound base for future physical and mental health is established. This information needs to be more widely known and understood.

References

1 H. B. Meire, 'Ultrasound measurements of fetal growth', in F. Falkner and J. M. Tanner (eds), *Human Growth* (Plenum Press, 1986).

2 Lux Flanagan, *The First Nine Months of Life* (Heinemann Medical Books, 1963).

3 D. R. Shanklin, 'Anatomy of the placenta', in F. Falkner and J. M. Tanner (eds), *Human Growth* (Plenum Press, 1986).

4 D. J. P. Barker and C. N. Martyn, 'The maternal and fetal origins of cardiovascular disease', *Journal of Epidemiology and Community Health* **46** (1992).

5 John Dobbing, 'Infant nutrition and later achievement', *Nutrition Review* **42** (1984).

6 Department of Health, *Dietary Reference Values for Food, etc.* (HMSO, 1991).

7 Ministry of Agriculture, Fisheries and Food, *Manual of Nutrition* (HMSO, 1985).

Chapter 4

PREGNANCY 2:
LOW-BIRTH-WEIGHT BABIES

The great majority (97 per cent) of babies are born normal and healthy but about 3 per cent suffer from a congenital disorder. I do not want to develop this much further; it is the low-birth-weight babies I want to concentrate on. Low birth weight is an indicator of many adverse influences during pregnancy, some of which could be cut out by the healthier habits mentioned in the last chapter. But 3 per cent of new-born babies is a great many, about 20,000 in 1988; and congenital anomalies account for one-quarter of deaths in the first year of life.

Parents love their children and when a mother gives birth to a handicapped child this may bring out qualities in the parents they thought they never possessed. Even so, congenital disorders create a heavy burden of illness on the child itself, with premature death sometimes being a possibility, and are a source of stress and strain in families. This is not to mention the huge emptiness left when a child dies.

Congenital disorders include some genetic conditions such as Down's syndrome (mongolism), and it is likely that the great majority of congenital anomalies, as well as much later ill-health, have a genetic base. Diabetes and high blood pressure are possible examples here.

Some congenital and genetic defects can be detected before or at birth (cystic fibrosis in the new-born and neural tube defect in the foetus), but most genetic disorders emerge during adult life. Judging from those present in adults of 25, 5–6 per cent of live-born infants carry a hidden genetic disorder, thus inflating the 3 per cent figure for congenital anomalies.[1]

Genetic defects are, in a strict sense, incurable. If those that carry them reproduce they may be handed down to all succeeding generations. With the greater understanding of diseases and their treatment, those that are affected may live to have children and thus the frequency of genetic disorders rises. Those who came to hospital to be cured now bring their children for cure. With the merciful decline in deaths from infectious disease the genetic diseases assume a greater frequency and importance in the population.

Abortion

Preventive measures to protect the foetus during pregnancy are largely in our own hands and have been mentioned. There is also a range of diagnostic techniques – ultrasonics, blood tests and others – which disclose a number of life-limiting congenital and genetic defects. The small minority of couples whose babies are affected have to make the painful choice either of giving birth to a child with risk of major impairment, with the disability and handicap it confers, or of choosing to terminate the pregnancy. But by *excluding* certain risks the tests can bring great relief.

Laws about abortion, as about anything else concerning morals or personal decisions, are blunt instruments and have little effect on human behaviour. Dr Johnson summed it up:

> How small, of all that human hearts endure,
> That part which laws or kings can cause or cure!

Freedom of choice on personal matters is right, though it needs a base of fact and a knowledge of alternatives and consequences.

Low birth weight

A baby may be born too soon, too small or both, with a weight below 2.5 kg, the internationally agreed definition of low birth weight (LBW). The average birth weight is about 3.5 kg. About 7 per cent of babies in the UK fall into the category of LBW but developing countries have a rate three or four times higher, while in a prosperous country with more uniform standards – Sweden, for example – only about 5 per cent of births are so classified.[2]

The reasons for low birth weight are complex but a distinction should be made between babies born *too early*, which is not harmful in itself (indeed most catch up), and those who for some reason or other have slow growth during the normal span of pregnancy.

In the UK, slow growth may be due to a variety of reasons, among them being lack of health in the mother due to poor circumstances in her own childhood, lack of ante-natal care, malformation of the placenta, smoking, alcohol, malnutrition, or something wrong with the baby itself. All these factors impinge on the health of the trio – mother, foetus, placenta – mentioned in the previous chapter.

In economically poor countries malnutrition is largely responsible for the high proportion of LBW babies. For whatever reason, children of LBW who are full-term are more likely to have some deficits in later size and mental ability. It now appears that a link exists between LBW, poverty, diabetes, and heart disease and stroke in later life (Chapter 10). On top of this, LBW increases the risk of death within 24 hours of birth, although better care has had a major impact on decline in LBW deaths. To reach a good birth weight is vital to a child's future well-being.

Smoking during pregnancy

In the UK, LBW is highest in the lowest social classes. These are the mothers who smoke the most, probably the most significant self-inflicted cause of LBW babies in the UK, perhaps because life presses on them harder than it does on others.

Recent evidence shows that mothers who smoke heavily (25-plus cigarettes a day) have, on average, babies with a 10 per cent deficit in birth weight (about 300 gms), a 2 per cent deficit in length at birth, and a 1.5 per cent deficit in head circumference compared with the babies of non-smokers. As the children grow up these effects decrease but residual effects in height are present up to at least 7 and probably beyond. There is a graded effect on all these aspects of growth depending on the number of cigarettes smoked.

The effects of smoking on height and later mental development may perhaps have a small nutritional element, not only because smoking reduces appetite but because smokers eat less fruit, meat and green vegetables compared with non-smokers.

Smokers also drink more tea with sugar in it, but the main reason for growth restriction is smoking.

Surprisingly, the precise factors in smoking which cause a slowing of growth of the foetus are not known, but carbon monoxide in smoke is under suspicion. Carbon monoxide from the mother's blood is taken up and probably concentrates in the baby's blood. Because carbon monoxide displaces oxygen in the blood, smoking reduces the amount of oxygen available to the baby's growing tissues and slows growth.[3]

Critical times

The sensitivity of the growing brain, nervous system, and other tissues and organs are great during pregnancy, as Chapter 3 made clear, and damage may be done by harmful habits. The child of a heavy smoker will not only be on average shorter but also backward in school work. Mothers who smoke ten or more cigarettes a day during pregnancy have children who are on average 3 to 5 months backward in reading, maths and general ability at ages 7 and 16 compared with the children of non-smokers,[3] but as a counterpoise these smoking mothers may have a life-style not conducive to interest in reading or books.

There is also the worrying physical evidence of smaller head circumference. Though the effects of smoking on head circumference are small, the effects on the brain and the development of brain cells could be considerable, but details are not available.

All the evidence with regard to physical health and mental development shows that it is of the utmost importance for parents to stop smoking during and after pregnancy, for the brain continues to grow fast up to ages 2 or 3 and will be sensitive throughout this period.

Smoking reduces birth weight, which is important to early survival. Perinatal morality (still birth and deaths in the first week of life) is increased by one-third by smoking.

Needs

Teachers, together with support from health visitors, can play a positive role in teaching the young what to do and what not to do in pregnancy. It should be stressed that many infant deaths and handicaps, as well as ill-health in adult life, are preventable by healthy life-styles in the mother. A nourishing and varied diet before pregnancy and from the earliest days of pregnancy is vital. An increased calorie intake is best avoided as it is unnecessary and contributes to obesity. Fruit and vegetables are very important for the health of mother and baby. Smoking, drug use and excessive alcohol during pregnancy all carry risks to the baby.

This teaching is particularly important in all areas but especially those of high risk such as inner cities. While the details of what is taught on this and many other subjects may be forgotten, windows are opened and years later that light may be useful.

References

1 Department of Health, *On the State of the Public Health for the Year 1988* (HMSO, 1989).
2 Pamela Davies, 'Maternal infection as a cause of low birthweight', *Maternal and Child Health* 14, no. 9 (1989).
3 Peter Elwood, P. Sweetham, O. Gray, D. Davies and P. Wood, 'Growth of children from 0–5 years: with special reference to mothers smoking in pregnancy', *Annals of Human Biology* 14, no. 6 (1987).

Chapter 5

THE FIRST YEAR OF LIFE

The infant and pre-school years from birth to 5 are crucial and form the genesis of a large proportion of what a person will be in health, behaviour and intellect in later years. Charles Darwin, when asked what period of life was the most formative time, replied: 'the first three years'.

They are years of rapid change and birth itself augurs change. It is sudden and traumatic because of the contrasts between life in the uterus and the outside world. The sudden change from a fluid to a gaseous environment, from a constant to a fluctuating temperature, from dependence on food from the mother's blood to food availability, are part of the shock of birth. The baby is also squeezed through the birth canal for several hours, during which the head is subject to much pressure, and it is intermittently deprived of oxygen because of the squeezing of the placenta and umbilical cord during contractions of the uterus. In addition to all this the baby produces very high levels of 'stress' hormones (adrenaline and noradrenaline) to help it to survive outside the uterus. The hormones clear the lungs, which assists normal breathing, mobilise food to nourish the body, and ensure that a good supply of blood goes to the brain and heart.

Despite this ordeal birth is largely free from damage, though it seems curious that the head should be in such an apparently vulnerable position during birth.

After birth a child grows faster than at any other time in life but not as fast as before birth, usually doubling its birth weight in the first six months and trebling it in a year. These are average figures and there is variation which is quite normal.

Although growth in height is falling in rate after birth it is still faster than at any other time in life. At aged 1 it is about 1.5 times the peak rate at puberty. The entire year fits the test of an exceptionally important critical period: a fast, though decelerating, rate of growth.

The speed of growth is, of course, relative. Compared with many other animals man is a slow grower in the uterus and after birth. A rat grows fast in the uterus and equally fast for a few months after birth, reaches maturity before a year and at 1 has increased its birth weight about 80 times. Its life span is about three years. All we manage is to treble our birth weight in a year and in eighteen years to multiply it twenty times.[1] Slow growth on our part relates to the lengthy time needed for learning. Man is not on a pedestal; the elephant is rather like us: mature at about 15, living to about 70, and in its way equally intelligent.

The achievement of large size depends on the *speed* of growing and on the *length* of time spent growing. A rat's life is short and fast, man's long and slow like the elephant's.

Returning to our own growth in the first year, weight loss may occur in the first month because food intake is low, but this is soon reversed. In fact, very little energy is needed to provide for the extra body tissue made in growing; maintenance and movement use most of the energy. Only about one-quarter of the energy intake is used for growing in the first month and 30 per cent in the second, but at six months it is down to about 10 per cent.[2] More and more is used for maintenance – that is, for maintaining life: breathing, heart beat, body temperature and so on – and for movement.

A rapidly growing infant will need a high percentage of protein but with increasing age and decelerating growth rate less dietary protein is needed for growth.

During this time the head, brain and sense organs are growing fast, as Chapter 1 explained. At birth the brain is 25 per cent of its adult weight, at six months it achieves about 50 per cent, reaching 60 per cent of adult weight at age 1. The brain is a 'gluttonous' organ and during its major growth spurt in the last three months of pregnancy and the first two years of life it uses protein fast. Estimates of brain growth at this time suggest a rate of 1 or 2 mg each *minute*.

Learning

Such fast growth can be seen as a preparation for rapid learning early on in life, but it is an odd fact of our own evolution that although the brain is man's special feature the delivery of the head is the most critical part of the trauma of birth.

At birth the most important part of the functional development of the brain starts at once, namely learning. The skin from all parts of the body begins to send messages to the brain in response to changes in temperature, contact with clothing, and with the mother's body and arms; and, of course, all the effects of gravity begin to operate fully for the first time. The only movements that are obviously fully established at birth are, as indicated in Chapter 3, the ability to breath, to suck and to swallow, all of which are strongly activated for survival and are 'hard wired' in the brain – that is, they can be done without teaching, with sucking and swallowing being individual actions which cannot take place at the same time.

The brain comes to receive more information through the eyes than from any other sense, but what is first seen has no meaning, and all light is dazzling and discourages eye-opening. Hearing is very active, however, but the new noises of hospital or home may be disturbing.

Limb movements are limited and crude, and are hampered by the clothing required in cold conditions. Nakedness is obviously best for freedom of movement, but this may be limited by climatic or housing conditions.

Unfolding abilities

From birth, children differ remarkably in the way they mature physically, mentally and emotionally, with each child going through the same order of development but at different rates. Thus, motor development (physical movement), language, social behaviour, and developments in thinking and feeling and in the senses, unfold, at least in the early years, to form some kind of pattern (see Table 6.1, pp. 50–4). In other words a child's capacity to walk, to talk, to learn and to respond to stimulation will all be determined by the maturity of certain nerve networks in the brain at particular ages. Premature babies, for instance, reach speech milestones at about the same time as babies born at normal time and stand and walk no sooner. There is much evidence that, in the brain, functions appear when brain structures mature and not before. As Tanner states, 'there is no reason to suppose that the truth of this generalisation suddenly ceases at two or three or 13'.[3]

One point of detail which has been referred to previously is the relatively late development of the legs in man. At birth the motor areas in the brain are most mature in the region controlling the upper trunk, neck and upper arm, then the leg and hand, and finally the head. By one month the hand has joined the rest of the arm and by three months the head has caught up and overtaken the legs. This order of maturity is maintained until about 2. The leg areas of the brain catch up at about 3 with the areas controlling the upper limb and head. By this age the infant is able to leave his mother to explore.

Similar unfolding happens in vision. A baby of a few days old will track a moving light if the speed is not too fast and as early as two weeks can tell the difference between a grey patch and a square composed of stripes that are only one-eighth of an inch wide, at a distance of nine inches from the face. At about four weeks certain parts of the brain have developed which allow fixation on the most salient elements in a pattern – the mother's eyes (because they have black and white contrast and move), or edges (where the hairline meets the forehead, for example). At about three months a mother's entire face is smiled at, not just the eyes. This is because the memory and visual parts of the brain have developed far enough to encode whole patterns and to form memory associations. The actual understanding of what a child sees gradually unfolds as the 'thinking' areas of the cortex mature. Indeed, as a general point it is possible that myelination of the higher parts of the brain may be very prolonged and associated with continually developing processes such as speech and abstract thought.

The brain's thinking areas

What are these 'thinking' areas in the brain? Most of the cortex at birth is like a 'blank slate' on which the lessons of experience will be written, including those of language. These blank, perhaps better expressed as 'thinking', areas probably store information and weave it into the mind. They occur in the enlarged frontal part of the cortex and large parts of the sides and back of the cortex. Certain parts of the left hemisphere endow us with the unique human quality, speech. The frontal parts, whose nature is poorly understood, probably give us the capacity to co-operate with others, for restraint in aggression and sexual capacities, and for thinking things out. Around the sensory, visual and auditory parts of the cortex are thinking areas associated with each. They help to give meaning to what is seen, heard or felt. If the vision-associated area is destroyed things can still be seen, but the meaning of what is seen is confused. These thinking areas give us what we call 'mind': the capacity for planned initiative, to choose, experiment, reason, imagine, and bring to speech what the person is.

What does all this matter in the first year of life? It is important to have high expectations of a baby's understanding from very early on because good interaction between mother and child leads to richer and richer communication. This is why talking to a baby early on face to face is important. More generally it is important to recognise that the quality of experience a child has, through stories, play and exploration, through love, trust and praise, is vital for the development of these blank areas of the brain. The experience will affect self-esteem for good or bad, enrich or impoverish the child as a person, and help or hinder in later schoolwork or in day-to-day behaviour. It is these thinking areas which give the human brain its openness and flexibility.

The notion of big areas of the cortex as a 'blank slate' to be filled with the lessons of experience is simple and should not mislead. The brain is living. Its potential for development is determined by heredity so that one person's brain will differ from another given the same experiences.

As a child grows he is formed gradually by the imprint of experience interacting with heredity. As he grows, his brain develops and strengthens its powers by practice and through the quality of experience provided. These properties are quite unlike those of a passive slate. It behoves parents and others to remember that the first year of life is the second great foundation stone after that of pregnancy. Its influence on the final structure is crucial.

Diet

During this remarkable first year when a child is developing and learning fast, an infant (boy) will need about 500 calories a day in energy and 13 gm of protein from birth to three months, a girl slightly less. At nine months to a year the need is for about 1,000 calories and 25 gm of protein a day, a bit less for girls. This is about a third of the energy requirements of a moderately active man.

Needless to say, good practices in infant feeding lay the foundations for a healthy child population. Breast-feeding is generally considered to be the best possible nutritional start for a variety of reasons. It is clean and all the nutrients are present in the right amount for human infants and in a readily absorbable form. Those nutrients that are low, such as iron and copper, are those which are already stored in large amounts in the infant's liver. Breast-feeding has the added bonus of protecting a child from certain diseases like gastro-enteritis during the first vulnerable months of life because the milk contains antibodies before the baby develops its own.

Babies have been fashioned to live on human milk and ideally a baby should have breast milk throughout the first year of life, supplemented by solid foods after four months. There has been official concern at the low level of breast-feeding in the UK, which in 1975 amounted to only 51 per cent at birth. It is now only 65 per cent, and only 20 per cent of mothers go on breast-feeding for nine months: society may find those odd who choose to go on longer!

The higher incidence of breast-feeding is associated with mothers who have been educated beyond 18, are of a high social class, living in London and the South-East, and who are over 25 and non-smokers.[4] I have remarked that LBW is more frequent in the poor. Once again the poor, for many complex reasons, are not providing the proper start for their children. Why? Is it because they do not know or have too many other pressures on them to bother? Perhaps the latter.

Malnutrition and learning

Malnutrition is unlikely to act alone to hamper early learning, acting instead in concert with other accomplices, both social and cultural. For example in developing countries such as Guatemala, mothers living in a primitive village who talked to their children in the local dialect, and who did not bother to listen to the radio, had infants whose weight at six months was significantly lower than children of mothers who listened regularly to the radio and used the national language in preference to dialect.[5]

Those mothers who do bother, as well as feeding their children properly, are more likely to provide a stimulating and diversified home environment compared with those mothers who stick to routine tradition.

Poverty in the UK pales beside this example, but signs of disadvantage – and fecklessness – are there in thousands of UK families: LBW, poor growth in infancy, lack of awareness of a child's needs early on. All of these are shaky foundations for later health and later development of mental potential at school.

Critical periods

The fast rate of growth and development in the first year and the swift development of the brain make this year a crucial time for mental, emotional and physical development and later adult health. Here are some proofs:

First, the effects of brain starvation just after birth at a critical time in development is illustrated by pyloric stenosis. Pyloric stenosis, with its onset at 21 to 30 days after birth, is sometimes associated with later intellectual defects, especially if the stenosis has caused weight loss greater than 10 per cent in expected body weight.

Second, one part of the brain grows earlier than the rest: the cerebellum, co-ordinator of fine muscular movement. Its growth spurt finishes about one year after birth while the rest of the brain continues its rapid growth. Besides lowering intellectual performance *chronic* malnutrition just after birth may cause children to be clumsier than normal, perhaps because of distortion of growth processes in the cerebellum during this critical time.[7]

Third, achievement of a good birth weight (3.5 kg or more) and a good weight at age 1 (12.3 kg or more) are beneficial to later health,[8] as Chapter 10 shows.

Fourth, as Chapter 1 explained, ethologists' observations and experiments with mammals and birds on bonding between mother and offspring show that the bonding process may have to start *immediately or very soon after birth* (witness the lost piping of young ducklings). It is argued by ethologists and some psychiatrists that disruption of the early phases in forming the first personal bond between mother and human child is the primary cause of failure in children to form personal bonds with the mother and, subsequently, social bonding of any kind. These bonds are formed and strengthened not simply by the presence of the mother or the mother-figure (the blood-tie is not of prime importance) who feeds the baby, but by an enormously subtle interaction between mother and child which involves eye-contact, touch (if a mother is left with her naked baby she touches each part of his body), the baby's cry, physical contact during breast-feeding, and facial expressions.

This delicately synchronised signalling and response between mother and child can be seen in the way a mother holds a baby, looks into its eyes, expresses mock-surprise saying 'ooooh' or affects the characteristics of a frown while the baby responds with signals and signs – smiling, gazing, grasping, babbling. This interaction is often terminated by the infant looking away and is likely to have been initiated by the mother on a cue from the infant that he/she is ready to respond.

In a human baby, however, attachment to one person, usually the mother, is likely to take place during the first year (the sensitive period) and not instantly, when the child is learning to discriminate. Indeed babies can attach to up to five people simultaneously and not necessarily always the mother, who is doing all the feeding and changing. This flexible attachment behaviour, in which a child learns that comfort and affection can come from several sources, has survival value (in an evolutionary sense), for such a child is likely to be more confident than a child who is afraid to leave his mother's knee. Babies take between seven and eight hours to attach in this flexible way.[9]

These facts on attachment behaviour have evolutionary advantage, for even after a 'bad start' in the first few months of life a child can recover and develop normal attachment behaviour, such is the plasticity and resilience of human behaviour. In fact, broadly speaking, the first year is a crucial time not only for forming a child's first love relationship, which provides the basic security and is a foundation stone of sound personality development, but for developing a whole range of signalling abilities (smiling, crying, clinging, and so on) that strengthen the bond between mother and child.

Needless to say, much more needs to be known about successful mothering and bonding behaviour. Experiences, both past and current, that help a woman to become a good mother, or those that make it more difficult, need clarifying. Does a woman's own experience of being mothered affect her ability (or lack of it) to be a successful mother?

Some mothers certainly have strong maternal feelings which enable them to achieve a firm bond of affection with their babies without difficulty, even after an initial period of separation. The strength of their maternal feelings may depend on the quality of mothering they themselves received in infancy.

In contrast, a mother may be unable to achieve this attachment without early close contact with her baby, and even then it may take a few days before the baby appears to her to be an individual and her own. Failure to form a normal attachment perhaps accounts for the higher incidence of 'battered babies' among babies who were initially separated from their mothers for long periods and among the infants of mothers who were themselves deprived of maternal attachment.

When a boy reaches the age of 1 he is about 44 per cent of his adult height, a girl about 46 per cent. The average weight for a boy is about 10 kg, for a girl about 9 kg. With height, the 'girls first' rule goes on and she reaches 50 per cent of adult height *on average* at 21 months compared with two years for a boy.[10]

The first year of life emerges from a host of studies as perhaps the most crucial period in the human span for the operation of environmental factors which influence growth, health and psychological development. This is perhaps the swiftest period of human learning, which is easily underestimated simply because a child then understands much more than it can say.

References

1 K. A. McCance and E. M. Widdowson, 'Glimpses of comparative growth and development', in F. Falkner and J. M. Tanner (eds), *Human Growth* (Plenum Press, 1986).

2 K. L. Bergmann and K. E. Bergmann, 'Nutrition and growth in infancy', in F. Falkner and J. M. Tanner (eds), *Human Growth* (Plenum Press, 1986).

3 J. M. Tanner, *Education and Physical Growth* (University of London Press, 1978).

4 Department of Health, *On the State of the Public Health for the Year 1988* (HMSO, 1989).

5 J. Cravatio and R. Arrieta, 'Nutrition, mental development and learning', in F. Falkner and J. M. Tanner (eds), *Human Growth* (Plenum Press, 1986).

6 S. R. Leeder and W. W. Holland, 'The influence of the environment on disease and growth in childhood', *Community Medicine* **1** (1978).

7 Roger Lewin, 'Malnutrition and the human brain', *World Medicine* **18**, no. 12 (1974).

8 D. J. P. Barker and C. Osmond, 'Infant mortality, childhood nutrition and ischaemic heart disease...', *Lancet* (10 May 1986).

9 J. P. Scott, 'Critical periods in organisational processes', in F. Falkner and J. M. Tanner (eds), *Human Growth* (Plenum Press, 1986).

10 J. M. Tanner, *Foetus into Man* (Castlemead, 1989).

Chapter 6

TWO TO FIVE: THE NURSERY YEARS

Even the most experienced nursery teacher is sometimes amazed at the achievements made intellectually, emotionally and physically by a normal child at a good nursery school or class. These attributes continue to advance rapidly in normal children at the infant stage also.

At the end of the last chapter I remarked that is is easy to underestimate children's intelligence before they begin to speak, yet on their part understanding is great. In anticipation of the words that will soon come at 12–18 months (see Table 6.1 for *average* times), jaw growth is enormous in the early months of life and at about one year it is already three-quarters of adult size. Talk is as vital as pure air to a child, and at home and in a good nursery school/class he should get plenty.

Linked with speech development will be use of the senses. The first of man's big achievements is learning to use these well in order to build up a knowledge of the world. At a good school children will get a variety of experience which will begin to develop their growing sensory powers. I want to return to the senses later but for the moment it is clear that children start school with different degrees of knowledge (of colours, for example) and different abilities. Some have wide experience and can relate well to others, speak clearly, draw, count, and a very few can turn a simple book into sense by reading it. At the other end of the scale some children, for a variety of reasons, have not begun to develop such competencies and depend heavily on others. This range of needs has to be taken into account in the work.

Once at school most children quickly learn to co-operate and respond positively to others; co-ordination and manipulative skills develop, as does language. Attention span is limited at

Table 6.1 How children's abilities develop: average milestones

Birth	In a few days follows moving objects with eyes. No colour vision. At about one month can fix on salient elements in a pattern – the mother's eyes.	Reacts to sound of human voice within a few days.	Fixes eyes unblinkingly on mother's face when feeding, reacts to familiar situations – feeds, baths. Smiles at strangers.
3 months	Lifts head, kicks vigorously, waves arms, hands loosely open.	Vision alert, interested in nearby faces. Follows adult movement near cot, recognises feeding bottle, and makes welcoming movements as it approaches face. Colour vision developing, but not complete. Whole face smiled at.	Coos, vowel-like sounds.
6 months	Sits, stands only with support, turns head from side to side to look	Moves head and eyes eagerly in every direction, follows an	Babbling, one syllable utterances, 'ma', 'da', 'de'.	Hands grasp for toys, takes everything to mouth, pats bottle when

Table 6.1 continued

round, holds arms to be lifted, kicks strongly, can roll over.	adult's movement across room, eyes seize on small interesting objects within 6–12 inches range – toy, spoon, uses whole hand in grasp. When toys fall out of cot forgets them. Can distinguish between face of mother and a stranger's.	feeding. Fear of strangers begins and shows slight anxiety or shyness if mother is out of sight, e.g. 'sobering' of face.
12 months Walks when hand held, crawls on feet and hands, sits on floor, may stand alone for a few moments, may walk alone.	Picks up small objects, (sweets) with precise pincer grasp of thumb and index finger, looks in correct place for toys which roll out of sight, points at objects he or she wants to handle. Outside, watches movements of people, cars, animals with	Definite single words, 'mamma', 'dadda', definite understanding of simple commands: 'Give it to Daddy', 'Say bye-bye'.
		Drinks from cup, chews, takes objects to mouth less, finds hidden toy quickly, likes to be in constant sight and hearing of adult, imitates (waving bye-bye, for example).

Table 6.1 continued

				intensity, recognises familiar people from twenty feet or more away.
18 months	Walks alone, sits on chair, pushes and pulls large toys, can carry teddy bear while walking, walks upstairs with help.	Builds tower of three cubes (hand), spontaneous scribble when given crayon and paper, enjoys simple picture book, turns two to three pages at a time, points to interesting objects out of doors.	Has repertoire of 3–50 word items, used singly but understands many more. No frustration if not understood, shows own hair, shoe, nose.	Drinks without spilling, holds spoon and gets food to mouth, explores environment energetically, remembers where objects belong, initiates simple activities – reading book, kissing doll, plays alone but likes adult to be near, still very dependent on mother.
2 years	Runs, walks up and down stairs two feet to a step holding on to rail or wall, climbs on furniture to look out of	Builds tower of six cubes. Spontaneous circular scribble and dots when given paper and pencil, enjoys	Vocabulary more than 80 words, two-word phrases, talks to himself/herself constantly when	Lifts and drinks from cup and replaces on table, chews completely, turns door handles, runs outside to

Table 6.1 continued

	Posture and large movements	Vision and fine movement	Hearing and speech	Social behaviour and play
	window or open doors, sits astride large wheeled toys and propels forward with feet on ground.	picture books, recognises detail, turns pages singly, recognises familiar adults in photograph after once shown. Colour vision fully developed.	playing, constantly asking names of objects, shows correctly and repeats words for hair, hand, feet, nose, eyes, mouth, shoe, on request.	explore, copies mother in domestic activities, defends own possessions, no idea of sharing, plays near older children but not with them.
3 years	Runs, operates tricycle, walks alone upstairs with two feet to step, can walk on tiptoe.	Builds tower of 9 cubes, copies circle, draws man with head (often with features), paints 'pictures' with large brush on easel, cuts with scissors.	Vocabulary of 1,000 words, grammar complex, gives full name and sex, talks about past experiences, asks many questions, knows several nursery rhymes.	Eats with fork and spoon, likes to 'help' in house and garden, much make-believe play, joins in play with other children, understands sharing, shows understanding of past and present.
4 years	Jumps over rope, catches ball, walks a line, walks up and down stairs one foot per step.	Builds tower of ten or more cubes, draws man with head, legs, features, trunk and often arms, copies cross, draws a simple house,	Language differs from adult only in style rather than grammar, gives name, sex, home address and often age, questioning, listens to	Eats skilfully with spoon and fork, strong dramatic play and dressing up, builds with boxes, planks outside, needs other

Table 6.1 continued

		matches and names four primary colours correctly. Spatial vision (detection of form) complete.	and likes long stories, often mixing up fact and fancy.	children to play with, understands taking turns, appreciates past, present and future.
5 years	Active and skilful in climbing, sliding, swinging, digging, dances to music.	Copies square, triangle and letters, draws recognisable man, draws house with chimney, door, windows and roof, counts fingers on one hand with index finger of other, names four primary colours and matches 10–12 colours. Binocular vision complete.	Speech fluent and grammatical. Gives full name, age and home address and usually birthday, loves stories and acts them out in detail later.	Uses knife and fork, domestic and dramatic play continued from day to day, co-operative, understands rules and fair play, tender and protective to younger children and pets.

Source: Adapted from various sources including *The Developmental Progress of Infants and Young Children* by Mary D. Sheridan (HMSO, 1975).

2, 3 and 4 and children change tack as interest catches them, but now and then they become absorbed and, for example, fit something together – perhaps for a long time. When they have achieved what they want the task is abandoned, almost as if they recognise their own limitations.

All of this can go in the wrong direction and stagnate into undemanding activities when ill-judged teaching, without intervention at the right time and without the adequate planning which is the backbone of a well-organised class, allows the children too much time to themselves to 'play'. But the normal drive in children is towards learning and in health their whole being is driven by curiosity and tireless energy.

Growth in young boys and girls

Patterns of growth in children are complicated and fairly well-defined but the rate of growth in height is falling sharply and levels off at about 4.

No prediction can be made at birth about a child's ultimate height because, as stated earlier, the size of a new-born baby reflects the environment in the mother's uterus and not its future pattern of growth. A boy may be born small but grow large because of his genetic endowment. Not all genes are active at birth and some begin to act only after a period of time. Perhaps this phased effect of genes lends support to the common observation that children grow to resemble their parents increasingly as they grow older.

At 4, the average boy is 58 per cent and at 5 is 62 per cent of his adult height so comparisons can be made. An average girl, always more advanced in her growth than a boy, is already 62 per cent of her adult height at four; 66 per cent at 5. The 'girls-first' rule is shown by the fact that she reaches 50 per cent of her adult height at 1.74 years compared with 2 years in a boy. There is so much variation among normal children, however, that this average information cannot be used to work out how tall a child will become when he or she is grown up.[1]

The growth curves of boys and girls from birth to about 5 differ slightly. At birth the average boy is growing a bit faster than a girl but the velocity equalises at about seven months.

After this the boys' rate of growth falls off more than the girls' until age 4, and from then on there is no difference until adolescence.

Infants born at the normal time have about 12 per cent of body weight as fat. Fat increases greatly in the first year of life. Girls are already a bit plumper than boys at birth, a trait that becomes more marked during childhood. But from about 1 to around 7 both slim down and become sturdier; muscle replaces fat as infants turn their attention from eating and growing to walking and playing. In the arm, for example, the circumference remains the same from 4 to 7 but the muscle/fat ratio changes in favour of muscle. The legs become longer relative to the trunk; the trunk lengthens relative to its breadth as well as to the size of the head. This trend continues up to puberty. In summary the pre-school and infant years are those in which the chunky physique of the new-born changes into the more elongated build of the child.

The increasing strength, spatial awareness and co-ordination of children of 4 and 5 allow them to run, jump, skip, climb and balance using a large range of climbing equipment as well as smaller apparatus and balls. Physical activity in play, in craft and in painting also develops the physical *control*, co-ordination and manipulative skills children will need in learning to write, a point taken up in Chapter 7.

A number of sex differences in growth patterns, quite apart from the reproductive organs, are present before puberty. Boys have longer and thicker forearms relative to upper arms and a boy's legs grow faster than the trunk just before puberty to give him relatively longer legs than a girl. The latter feature is mainly due to the longer period of pre-adolescent growth in boys.

Change in height is normally taken as an overall measure of growth, but in man this masks the remarkable pattern of differential growth which is commented upon in Chapter 1. Up to puberty the brain and head, including the sense organs, are nearer their final size than the body and it is only during and after the adolescent growth spurt, at about 18 or 20, that the body catches up. Thus at the age of 5 the brain and head are about 80 per cent grown, the body only about 40 per cent.

Diet

During the early school years children are active and growing, and compared with adults their energy and nutrient needs are high in relation to their size. The Department of Health's daily food recommendations for a 4-year-old girl are: for energy 1,500 calories, for protein 37 gm and for thiamin 0.6 mg. These are about 70 per cent of those required for a grown woman. For 4-year-old boys they are about half those of a moderately active man.[2]

At about 7, a child's need for calcium is greater than that of a grown-up. Too little calcium in the bodies of young children results in stunted growth and rickets. It is the most abundant mineral in the body and all but 1 per cent of it is in the bones and teeth. The remainder is crucial for contraction of muscle including heart muscle, for proper nerve conduction and for normal blood clotting. Milk and cheese and, in this country, bread-and-butter puddings contain significant amounts of calcium. The main source of calcium for all children though is liquid milk which contributes over one-third of calcium requirements for 10-year-olds and no doubt for younger children as well.

During the period of rapid growth in infancy a sufficient supply of vitamin D is important for the calcification of bone. Vitamin D achieves this mainly by facilitating the absorption of dietary calcium from the intestine. It may be necessary to supplement this vitamin in the winter months up to the age of 5 and in children where there is a risk of malnutrition from either inadequate or unbalanced diets. Care has to be taken because overdose of vitamin D is dangerous; it causes too much calcium to be absorbed and the excess is deposited, with consequent damage.

Margarine and many milk products are fortified with vitamin D but fatty fish is also a good source. Lack of vitamin D causes the development of rickets. Vitamin D is obtained both from the action of sunlight on the skin and from the diet, with the former being the main source. It is important here to remember that Asian children, because of customs of dress and by remaining indoors, may develop rickets, so that good sources of vitamin D need to be available in their diet in supplements.

Besides lack of vitamin D some immigrant groups who remain on traditional diets may lack iron. Hindus are mostly vegetarian and fish is rarely eaten; Muslims eat 'halal' meat (meat that is completely bled at the time of slaughtering). A fifth of the iron in the British diet comes from meat (from which it is readily absorbed), but bread, flour, potatoes and vegetables (and curry powder) contain iron which is, of course, important in the constitution of blood. More than half of the iron in the body is in the form of haemoglobin and lack of it will cause anaemia. Normally only about 10 per cent of dietary iron is absorbed from the food though when the body's stores are depleted and when needs are greatest, as in growing children, iron absorption increases. A great deal of the daily diet of children (except older boys) is below the recommended amount for iron. For 2–5-year-olds this is about 2–5 mg/day.[2]

Critical periods and school

Senses

I noted in the last chapter how rapidly the brain comes into action after birth and commented then on the pattern of development of the motor and visual areas of the grey matter (cortex). Detailed knowledge of the brain is sparse and is rather like an old map, though some general areas are becoming known. It would be a great help for teaching and learning if a detailed map existed for then we should know when best to teach something and how. All this is still in the distant future but a little is known about the development of the senses, of logic, speech, and a sense of pattern – all basic to the growth of intellect.

Aristotle taught that what is in the mind is first in the senses. Few of us, especially in the TV age, have developed all our senses as fully as we might but the drive to develop them comes at birth and continues right through the critical times of the pre-school and primary years. Along with the drive (and necessary to it) is the urge to find out. To feed curiosity and use the pre-set precious time well a child needs to handle different textures, shapes and weights and needs colours to sort.

Detailed maps already exist for some of the *senses*, but they only give access to the foothills of understanding. Vision, for example, has some detailed bits mapped, but how colour, depth, motion, texture, and orientation combine into an image of a face in our consciousness is unknown.

In vision there is a series of overlapping sensitive times for the development of various visual attributes in the rhesus monkey and they may be similar in ourselves. In the monkey the period for the development of perceived dim light is three months, for colour and bright light six months, for spatial vision or detection of form about a year, for binocular vision more than a year. J. M. Tanner[1] suggests that over this age range the ages in rhesus monkeys may be converted to human equivalents by multiplying by four. So for a child, colour vision is developed by about 2, spatial vision by 4 and binocular vision (depth vision) by 4 or 5.

Hand in hand with these developing visual attributes, co-ordination and fine and large movements unfold as brain structures gradually mature (see Table 6.1).

These unfolding powers mean that, during the nursery years, work with colours, spatial activities through movement in a variety of settings, and the use of tools for simple design work are all fully in order for most children of 4 or 5. This is done in many nursery and reception classes. Children of 4 use screwdrivers, pliers and sandpaper to 'mend' equipment, and small hacksaws (with necessary safety devices to prevent wood slipping) to make models. These activities also help children to develop the co-ordination and manipulative skills they need in handwriting.

I have noted the experiments on critical times in vision with kittens in Chapter 1; with ourselves we have only the crudest evidence for their timing and length, but there are a few pointers. People who have been born blind but have later gained sight are able to see only a swirling mass of colour. With time they may learn to see – and understand what they see – but it is a lengthy and difficult process quite unlike the normal acquisition of vision at the right time by a child. More specifically the brain is vulnerable to the effects of abnormal vision such as squint and astigmatism up to about aged 6 or 7. Damage to sight is hard to put right after 7 and squint after 7 because the visual system has passed through its critical time of development by then and the pattern of nerve connections is abnormal. It is therefore absolutely vital to detect visual (and auditory) handicaps at *2 years old or earlier* to prevent later handicap.

Touch

Whether there are similar sensitive periods for the development of hearing, touch, taste and smell is not known but they are likely. It is certainly so in rats.

With regard to touch, children have much visual experience through television but perhaps not enough experience of touch. Therefore, it is good to see young children at nursery and infant school experimenting with texture, which is important and fascinating to them. They soon begin to learn the differences between a smooth surface and a whole variety of other surfaces. People are marvellously adapted for active rather than passive touch because we can learn more about the world by having the nervous system so adapted. If shapes are pressed into the palm of the hand (passive touch) they are less accurately identified than if they are accessible to exploration by the fingertips (active touch). Children's exploring fingers are an extension of their eyes or vice versa.

I mentioned earlier, in Chapter 5, that certain parts of the cortex are devoted to each of the senses. For touch, which I have just referred to, there is much more space on the grey matter devoted to the face, especially the lips, and to thumbs and fingers than to the trunk. In the pig, the touch area, linked to the snout, is as big as the visual cortex. Our fingers are as important to us for exploration as its snout is to the pig.

Children who are encouraged to experiment with the senses by handling things different in shape, texture and weight, using objects to shake and bang, listening to music, mixing and sorting colours, having things to taste and smell, are learning to see, touch, hear, smell and taste and to discriminate. Much of this experience comes from *purposeful* play, which is not a free, totally unstructured activity but one which is planned so that children encounter the experiences intended.

Play that is well-planned and that children enjoy provides the solid base to improve their language competence.[3] It also helps them to learn how to think. Children under about 5 can only really think by doing, looking, listening and touching, and the environment has to be conducive to this. Adults, even when they are idle, have their thoughts to keep the brain active. Children need to play to pep up the brain and to keep it primed and active until they themselves acquire the capacity for 'internal thinking'. Those who despise play as wasteful of time are wrong. It has been evolved as a strong part of human make-up and has survival value. Learning to think is one asset of play. Another is helping a young child to find out what it feels like to be someone else (by pretending to be a mother, a father and so on) which is a step towards another basic human attribute: the need to co-operate.

Speech

Just as the development of vision seems to have a key phase, speech development has its own critical time – from birth to about 8 or 10. There is no better start to language than the daily life of a good home. Meal times, washing, dressing, the mother's talk, outings and plans introduce a child to a range of experiences, language and voice. Many children of 3 and 4 already use language flexibly and for a variety of purposes (see Table 6.1). Good pre-school education encourages this for children to extend and use their skills. Some children at this age are not lucky. No one listens to them or talks to them or shares the delights of experience. They enter school at 5 deprived and with poor vocabularies.

If a child hears no speech for the first 8 or 10 years of life it is very likely that if taught later he or she will speak only with great difficulty and be very retarded. This is dealt with in detail in the next chapter but meanwhile I want to show that the brain is poised to learn speech and that all it needs is words to set the machinery in motion. This inevitability of learning to speak by imitation in this critical period which starts at birth is strikingly shown by two children brought up by their deaf-mute grandmother in the last century in a remote area of Jutland. The children conversed fluently in a language no one could understand and which had no similarity to Danish![4]

What special features of the brain make a young child a specialist in learning to speak? First, a simple observation of the brain of a new-born baby shows that the left half of the cortex, where language is usually developed, is bigger than the right half. It is possible, though not proved, that this enlarged area represents an internal machinery designed to learn speech from birth. If electrodes are placed over this 'speech bump' of infants a month old, and over a corresponding area on the right side of the head, there is greater electrical activity over the left hemisphere when words and syllables are played. This confirms that the left hemisphere is very sensitive early in life to speech sounds.[5]

Next, the parts of the brain in the motor cortex which help to give delicate control to the tongue, jaws and lips are large in proportion to the parts that control movement in other parts of the body. Six times more grey matter is made over to the lips than to the whole trunk. This distortion is a reflection of the importance of speech in our daily lives.

A baby coos, gurgles and smiles long before it can speak, but despite the lack of speech it understands plenty. As every mother knows, understanding shines in its eyes, while excitement at a word – 'Daddy' – shows in its kicking and gestures. This is because the delicate brain machinery for *understanding* speech develops earlier than the parts for uttering speech. At 18 months to 2 years, on average, children will use around 50 words with meaning and link words into simple sentences; but before that they can understand much of what is being said to them. This is why we should talk to a baby early. It is only by assuming that a baby understands and has the necessary intelligence that it will learn to speak and think.

Microscopic examination of certain parts of the cortex shows a dramatic increase in the branching of nerve cells between 15 and 24 months. It is as if the brain is building up to a springboard of nerve development from which speech can take off.

At nursery school, it is clear that on average girls are ahead in their speech development between 3 and 5, and it is likely that the speed of nerve development is greater in the speech 'bump' of 4-year-old girls than in that of boys. Because girls and ahead in their speech development pre-school they may be more disadvantaged than boys if talk is impoverished at home because they pass through their sensitive time for language development somewhat earlier. The early reliance on speech by girls also has a bearing on learning mathematics and science; this is taken up in the next chapter.

Because the brain is hidden and complex there is still a mystery about how we learn speech and how the brain processes it. The most stunning achievement of all, and one not in the least understood, is how a child moves on from the mere learning of words as they are specifically taught, to putting them into combinations never before said or heard which are understood by the listener; and later uttering the same words again but in new combinations. It all must mirror ripening of brain structures about which we as yet know little.

It was Walter de la Mare who wrote: 'It is a very odd thing, as odd as can be, that whatever Miss T eats turns into Miss T.' This observation applies to what is heard and its quality. So it is important to talk to a child from birth. It is as vital to the development of the brain and intellect as fresh air and good food is to general health. Shutdown answers and questions that require one-word answers – 'yes' and 'no' – harm the development of language after its natural onset. Discussion strengthens both language and general mental development.

From a very early age a child should be encouraged to explain, select, or simply recount experiences. Then knowledge will become well-rooted in thought and in language instead of possessing but a frail hold and being rapidly forgotten. He should also be encouraged to ask questions and to hear exact answers. Learning new words through discussion and listening will also help a child to respond to demands with precision. Once a name of an object is heard a child notices with delight a particular element in the environment which before went unnoticed.

Sometimes silence is the best help with chidren of all ages. Too much well-meant interference with tedious explanations and books can destroy the silent sensory pleasures of looking, feeling, smelling and listening.

Logic

Most nursery and infant schools regard talking and listening to individual children as one important duty. If listened to carefully they are often devastatingly logical. Even when something vanishes behind a screen, a 1-year-old will probably know where it is, even though it cannot be seen. This remarkable capacity of the baby and young child to 'reason' modifies some of the theories of the past about children's thinking. It is held by Jean Piaget that not until between 7 and 9 does a child develop powers of logical analysis. It enables the inference that if one thing is bigger than a second and the second is larger than the third, then the first must be bigger than the third. On the other hand, if children of 5 or 6 are shown two sticks whose height is equal, but one is further away than the other, they typically judge the further one as smaller. But children of 4 and 5 can reason deductively if the situation is a real-life one and is not a contrived laboratory experiment. Observation of children in natural situations is likely to tell us more. Thus Margaret Donaldson[6] cites comments children make and questions they ask when they listen to stories. Here are a couple of examples:

1　'But how can it be [that they are getting married]? You have to have a man too.' [The book contains an illustration of a wedding in which the man looks rather like a woman. The child thinks it is a picture of two women.] (*Premises:* 1 You need a man for a wedding; 2 There is no man in the picture. *Conclusion:* It can't be a wedding.)
2　*Child:* 'You're not looking.'
　　Teacher: 'Pardon?'
　　Child: 'Why are you not reading it?'
　　Teacher: 'Because I know it.'
　　(*Premises:* 1 When you read a book you look at it; 2 The teacher

is not looking at the book. *Conclusion:* She is not reading the book.)

So at least from the age of 4 it must be acknowledged that the supposed gap between children and adults in reasoning power is less than many people have claimed. Other modern work supports this view.

What is happening inside the grey matter to accompany these growing capabilities of the mind is unknown, except that the nerve cells in the cortex grow and form a rich network of branches from birth onwards. Perhaps the richness of branching of the nerve cells and their millions of interconnections are important in the development of intelligence. But for practical purposes a normal child of 4 or 5 entering a nursery or reception class has a brain which in certain circumstances is capable of thinking logically, an attribute that requires a high level of skill and knowledge in the teacher to foster and sharpen. Neglect of this critical period of development by policy-makers has damaged the progress of thousands of children through lack of good nursery schools and classes.

Pattern

Appreciation of pattern and order seems to be basic in human development and children of 4 or 5 look for patterns to help explain their world. To go deeper, it suggests that the brain is not haphazard in scanning the world but searches for order. The significance of pattern and order to a child is shown at nursery and infant school by often tireless crayoning of borders to a picture or a story book, or by the child making all-over coloured patterns.

The search for order is shown if a child is watched painting. When children paint a picture of Mum it seems to follow a kind of pattern. Head, arms, legs, the units of a painting, seem to be painted in sequence and the sequence changes with age. Children move from top to bottom and left to right. A 3-year-old will paint Mum as a circle with some face details, thin legs coming out of her head. Some of them stop there to leave armless figures. But the crucial point is this: others after a look go back 'to finish', to add ears, arms and other detail. By

5 the whole figure is there, trunk and all. The 5-year-old has learned to put the parts together. Nevertheless the 3-year old must *know* what his or her mother looks like but cannot yet assemble the parts.

The child who 'goes back to finish' seems to have become adept at running an eye over the painting to see if all the pieces are there – eyes, limbs and so on.

Looking for patterns is at the heart of science and mathematics (taken up again in the next chapter), and this search for pattern and order should be encouraged by many simple tasks: positioning chairs round a table, laying it with cutlery, arranging flowers and homely activities that encourage looking and constructing and give satisfaction in a job well done. Let a 3-year-old watch you write. He will scribble his own version across the page and seems to be aware that to write is to make flowing rhythmic bands of pattern. When reading him a story show him whole words in the book and he will recognise the word pattern again. He will enjoy and remember 'elephant' better than 'this' or 'is'. Tell him nursery rhymes, number jingles and simple poems and stories. His memory will retain the order and pattern. If you miss a word by mistake in a family story he will soon fill it in, gleefully correcting you.

Three: a crucial turning point

Turning to an important behavioural pattern, in Chapter 1 I stressed that attachment behaviour is probably based on a critical pattern of growth that proceeds rapidly, falling afterwards to a low level but never quite stopping. Bonding is intense between mother and child in the first critical year, as Chapter 5 explains, but the nursery years show that 'attachment behaviour' is still developing and that this time is also critical though perhaps at a lower level of intensity. These developments coincide with the brain spurt and may link with an epoch when young nerve cells are plastic in widespread areas of the brain and are able to respond to the environment by altering their connections.

When children are separated from their mother and other familiar figures for a prolonged period, or repeatedly during the *first three years of life*, which seem to be quite critical, 'detachment' behaviour (despair, anxiety) can persist indefinitely.[7] This has particular relevance in relation to mothers returning to work. Children who have reason to be confident that 'attachment figures', like mother or another loved person, will be available to them when they need them are less prone to anxiety than those who lack reasons for such confidence. This confidence, or the lack of it, in knowing that mother and other loved people will be there when wanted, is established during the first three years of life and tends to persist relatively unchanged throughout life. Good mothering and a secure, happy home life form the basis for an inner sense of security in later life. All these facts have precise similarities in the behaviour of the young of other species of primates. All the impressive evidence simply reinforces what the majority of parents and nursery teachers know by instinct and common sense.

But there is an important difference between man and other primates that has relevance to schooling. By the age of 3, provided he knows where mother is and has good reason to believe that she will come back soon, a child begins to accept another fairly familiar person (a nursery teacher) even when he is in a not too familiar place. By 3 a human child can talk with his mother and understand the message 'back later'. His memory will tell him that this has happened before and everything is all right. She will be back. His mother will have brought him to school and remained with him for an hour the first time or two while he explored in her presence, staying in his sight and within reach of his voice. His confidence has built up and his brain says that the situation is reasonable. But mother must come back or he will begin to lose confidence.

Long or repeated separation from her before the age of 3 can give rise to persistent anxiety and insecurity for she needs to be both accessible and responsive to his needs. It was Sigmund Freud who said 50 years ago that 'anxiety in children is originally nothing other than an expression of the fact that they are feeling the loss of the person they love'.

What about working mothers and the spin-off on the child? The evidence is not clear-cut one way or the other but recent studies stress that if a mother is happy and satisfied at work, the children are better adjusted than if a mother is frustrated by not working. Contented mothers, working or not, seem to produce the happier child. But, of course, in this instance the quality of the substitute care the mother is able to arrange is critical.

Provision

Of the under-fives receiving education in maintained provision it is unfortunate that only approximately 24 per cent are in nursery schools or designated nursery classes and units, while 21 per cent go to primary school classes.[8] Most of those admitted early to primary school are 4 years old. Some authorities have traditionally admitted children early but as rolls have fallen and space has become available this practice has now become more widespread, and most now admit children before they reach statutory school age. The most common practice is to admit children at the beginning of the school year in which they are 5.

The latest statistics show that as many as 62 per cent of 4-year-olds are in infant classes. Some are in reception classes alongside older children within the same year group; others are taught with children aged 5 and 6 years and, sometimes, with 7-year-olds. Unfortunately, the work done in the infant classes by nursery age children is too often narrow, undemanding and wasteful of this critical time.

Taking all factors into account, children under 5 in nursery schools and classes generally receive a broader and better-balanced education than those in primary classes. The work is well planned, with a good emphasis on purposeful play and exploratory activity. Other conditions associated with the more frequent occurrence of better-quality education in nursery schools and classes include: a narrower age band of children; better adult/child ratios; accommodation which in the main is purpose-built, or well-adapted to the age group; better material resources; and more teachers experienced in teaching 3- and 4-year-old children.

For many years the wisdom of admitting 4-year-olds – and even younger children – to infant classes has been questioned.

It is a policy which is fair neither to the younger children nor to those of statutory school age; and it is wasteful of a period which is of outstanding importance intellectually. Indeed, thousands of children have no chance of ever developing their powers to the full because good nursery schools and classes are unavailable to them. None of this should diminish the importance of a child-minder, perhaps *potentially* the best type of day care for the pre-school child, not the worst.[9] A homely atmosphere with a small group of children from different backgrounds might provide the best learning environment for very young children and good use of a vital critical time.

References

1 J. M. Tanner, *Foetus into Man* (Castlemead, 1989).
2 Ministry of Agriculture, Fisheries and Food, *Manual of Nutrition* (HMSO, 1985).
3 Niko Tinbergen, 'Functional ethology and the human sciences', *Proceedings of the Royal Society (B)* **182** (1972).
4 O. Jesperson, *Language: Its Nature, Development and Origin* (Allen & Unwin, 1922).
5 J. H. Harris, 'Sex differences in the growth and use of language', in E. Donaldson and J. Gullahorn (eds), *Women: A Psychological Perspective* (Wiley, 1977).
6 Margaret Donaldson, *Children's Minds* (Fontana, 1978).
7 John Bowlby, *Separation, Anxiety and Anger* (Hogarth Press, 1979).
8 DES, *The Education of Children under Five* (HMSO, 1989).
9 A. F. Osborn and J. E. Milbank, *The Effects of Early Education* (Oxford University Press, 1987).

Chapter 7

THE PRIMARY SCHOOL YEARS

Unspectacular but steady growth, with height gains of 6 to 7 cm a year up to age 5, and 5 to 6 cm up to age 10, marks this stage of development. In many children there is the 'mid-childhood' spurt between 6 and 8, and its small bump can be seen in Figure 1.2b (see Chapter 1). The steadiness of general growth in these years masks the pattern of differential growth, for at 5 the brain and head are 90 per cent of adult weight with the body having reached 40 per cent of its final weight. At 11, or thereabouts, the body is around half its adult size, the brain and head fully grown. These bare facts conceal the rapid development of manual and bodily dexterity during these years and the speed of mental development – all of which I shall return to in a moment.

If one looks at snapshots of, say, top infants and of top and middle juniors, the physical changes are marked (see Photographs 1, 2 and 3). Boys and girls in the top infant class are much the same in build, though boys are generally a shade taller, less plump and more muscular. In the top junior class the position is reversed. Girls are a shade taller, heavier and often stronger than boys – though boys expect to be all of these, but are not. Some girls of 11 will be physically advanced, having had their first menstrual periods perhaps at 10½. So children in top juniors will consist of two disparate groups: girls who have started to develop and boys who remain small boys.[1]

Though these years are fairly unspectacular in growth rates, there is a steady change in the various proportions of the body. The legs continue to become longer relative to the trunk, and the trunk lengthens relative to its breadth as well as to head size.

This bare description conceals changes in fat and muscle.[2] From the age of 6 or 7 there is a gradual increase in body fat

Photograph 1 Infants aged 5/6. *Chronological* age is convenient simply because it is exactly known but it tells little that is important about a child and conceals much that is vital at all ages. At this age most children can skip, jump, climb well, run, balance and use a range of tools correctly and safely. They are developing the co-ordination and manipulative skills needed in learning to write. Note the children's body proportions: relatively short legs and large head in proportion to height, and the chunky forearms of the boys. Leg length at this age makes children relatively poor at leaping and running fast.

in girls which continues through puberty. The gap in total body fat between girls and boys is considerable and persists. Girls of 9, for example, have an average of about 16 per cent of body weight as fat, boys 12 per cent. Twelve-year-old girls have about 22 per cent of body weight as fat, boys 18 per cent. The puppy fat which embarrasses some girls at adolescence gives them feminine curves and even at 12 increases their sexual attractiveness before they are mature enough to be interested in the opposite sex. After puberty the average adult male has around 12 per cent body weight as fat, the average female, 25 per cent.

The proportion of muscle tissue remains more constant in both sexes, contributing more weight in boys than in girls of

Photograph 2 Junior children aged 8/9 running. Now most children are well co-ordinated physically. Note the proportions of the body in this and later photographs compared with the infants in Photograph 1. Children have longer legs and comparatively shorter bodies. In consequence the power to run and leap increases markedly throughout the primary school. Head size is smaller now in proportion to height.

all ages. At 5, for example, boys have about 42 per cent muscle, girls 40 per cent. By 9 boys have 46 per cent, girls 42 per cent, and by 13 boys have 46 per cent, girls 43 per cent. Puberty markedly changes muscle composition in the sexes and adult men have around half their weight as muscle, while women have 40 per cent.

Strength and co-ordination

These changes – legs becoming longer, bodies comparatively more compact, development of physical strength – increase the power to run and to leap between the ages of 5 and 11. There is little difference between the sexes in strength, agility and balance. Arm thrust and pull is similar, strength of leg muscles is no different until after adolescence when boys' arm and calf muscles are much wider and stronger. The marked sex difference is strength of hand grip, boys having the

Photograph 3 Top juniors aged 10/11. Note the long legs and relatively compact bodies which enable good leaping and running at this age. Their natural agility and imagination give children at this stage the power to perform antics, climb, sit and crouch, in extraordinary ways. Note the differences in muscular development of the forearms between boys and girls.

stronger grip from about 9 or 10. This fact recalls the sex differences in forearm strength mentioned in Chapter 6.

Co-ordination of hand and eye improves steadily throughout the primary years. Children of 5 often have difficulty in catching or hitting a ball though they may throw surprisingly well. At 10 or 11 they are much more skilful.

It is always difficult to judge when children are ripe for specific instructions in specific skills. One or two indications suggest that it is important not to try to attempt learning any activity before the age at which success is possible. In a study of twins (thought to be identical but later proved not so), one twin could be taught to swim and roller-skate at a very early age even before he could walk well but showed no advance over the other twin when retaught at a later age. In fact roller-skating proved more difficult because it had been learned at an age when the proportions of leg length and body length were different from the earlier period and the skills had to be relearned.

Judging from electrical patterns obtained by electroencephalogram (EEG), brain development seems complete about 8, though there is plenty of normal variation and it is about this time that most children first begin to be well co-ordinated physically. This facility should be predictable at a time when the nervous system, sensory abilities and motor organs – legs, arms, etc. – are close to adult form.[3] It looks as if the period of the later part of the mid-growth spurt (about 8) is one in which to initiate the development of physical skills – ice-skating, for example, which requires split-second co-ordination, and the learning of difficult instruments like the violin and oboe, although of course hand-span is important.

With regard to physical education, children's development makes them able to leap high and far and run fast at 11 whereas at 5 they are feeble at leaping but good at climbing. At the primary stage children are still very mobile (anatomically) though less so than a baby who can suck its toes. Nevertheless this mobility allows primary children to assume attitudes, perform antics, and make movements which may surprise. Any PE programme therefore needs to give weight to activities of an athletic kind which require strength and also those of an expressive kind which also require co-ordination and imagination. The younger the child the more intertwined are the two. Equally, a balance is necessary between co-operation and competition, and, most important, work which recognises individual progression.

Children at the top of the primary school have largely outgrown the typical school hall and much of the apparatus provided in it.

I will pick up the importance of regular exercise to good health in Chapter 11.

Diet

Turning to diet, schoolchildren in the 5–11 range are growing fast though not as fast as after birth or at puberty. They 'burn' more fiercely than older children or adults. Their hearts beat faster, their metabolic rate is higher and cuts heal swiftly. They are like darting swallows rather than steady grey mares.

Because of their smaller size compared with adults – and correspondingly smaller stomachs – meals should be little and often. They have big appetites which reflect need rather than greed but this does not mean 'grazing' on biscuits, sweets, cakes and crisps all day long but rather developing sensible eating habits.

But what do children actually eat? Information on children's eating habits is scattered and scanty, especially for 5–8-year-olds. As HMI I looked for myself at school meals, tuck shops and the contents of lunch boxes and formed some impressions of what is eaten rather than what theorists suggest might be. These observations do not replace detailed surveys, which again supply facts rather than theories. One recent survey of the weekly diet of 300 schoolchildren by the Department of Health has just been published.[4] It deals with 10/11- and 14/15-year-olds. I shall use some of the data for the younger age group at this point as having some bearing on the diets of primary children.

It should be remembered that the 1980 Education Act released local authorities from the need to conform to pre-scribed nutritional standards and left them free to decide the form, content and price of school meals. Prior to this Act it had been laid down that a school meal should provide a minimum of one-third of the recommended daily intake of energy and between one-third and one-half of the recommended daily intake of protein. Ministers agreed, prior to the new arrangements, that they should be monitored, hence the survey.

The dietary survey just mentioned shows that British schoolchildren are taller and heavier than ever before and there is no evidence of general undernutrition. Average energy intakes are about 90 per cent of the 1979 DHSS Recommended Daily Amount (RDA) but there is no indication that the intake is inadequate. It rather suggests that children are less active than their predecessors.

On average, 10-year-old boys are 142.8 cm tall, and girls 142.9 cm. The standard heights measured by J. M. Tanner in 1959 and adjusted in 1965 were 139.3 and 139.5 cm, respectively, for boys and girls of 10. Weights on average are 36.8 kg for boys and 37.1 kg for girls compared with the earlier stan-dards of 31.9 and 33.0 kg. Younger primary children have risen similarly in proportion.

The main sources of dietary energy in children's food over the space of a week are bread, chips, milk, biscuits, meat products, cakes and puddings. The most frequent foods eaten are chips, crisps, cakes and biscuits. Boys eat more chips, breakfast cereals and baked beans than girls and drink more milk. Girls eat more fruit and drink more fruit juice than boys. Yoghurt, fizzy drinks (half a litre a week on average) and sweets (90 gm per day on average) are more popular among the 10- than the 14-year-olds, with the younger children claim-ing to eat biscuits and cakes every day.

An 8-year-old boy requires about 2,000 calories a day, a girl slightly less. The boy's protein requirements are about 50 gm/day, a girl's about the same. These are about two-thirds the needs of moderately active men and very close to the needs of the 'average' woman. Calcium needs are about the same as those for 4-year-olds mentioned earlier, with iron needs being a bit higher at 10 mg/day.[5]

With regard to school meals, 10-year-olds (and presumably younger children) obtain over half their bun and pastry intake, and between 30 and 40 per cent of their chips, from school dinners. There is no great difference between the average energy or nutrient content of children eating school meals from a free-choice cafeteria-style system and those eating a fixed price–fixed menu meal. The school meal contributes between 30 and 43 per cent of the daily energy intake and so fulfils one of the old pre-1980 Education Act requirements.

The main energy sources in diets were given a moment ago. For 10-year-olds protein represents about 12 per cent of this energy intake, fat about 38 per cent, and carbohydrate the remaining 50 per cent. The average of 38 per cent fat conceals the fact that one-quarter to one-third of children eat foods which contribute more than 40 per cent of their energy intake as fat and three-quarters eat foods which contribute more than 35 per cent. These proportions are at odds with the official recommendation that total fat intake should not exceed 35 per cent of energy, as a preventive measure against heart and arterial disease. Half the fat in the diets of children of all ages is obtained from milk, chips, meat products, biscuits, carcass meats, crisps and butter, but milk makes the single largest contribution to fat intake in 10-year-olds (12 per cent fat intake) with chips next (8 per cent).

My casual observations as HMI are that fatty foods are chosen at cafeteria meals despite lessons on healthy eating. During inspections I have seen an individual boy or girl choose chips on several consecutive days (and sometimes nothing else), followed by a bun and a fizzy drink. Standard dinners also contain too much fat and not enough fresh fruit and vegetables at both primary and secondary schools.

Packed lunches are, of course, variable. The dietary survey shows, as expected, that 10-year-old boys taking a packed lunch, compared with those eating other kinds of lunch, eat the most bread, biscuits, margarine, cheese, crisps and apples. Similarly, girls of 10 eat more yogurt, cheese, crisps and fruit, and drink more fruit juices and soft drinks than girls consuming other types of lunch.

My observation of infants' lunch boxes quite often showed that too much was given and wasted, and that white bread and butter sandwiches were fairly common, together with a chocolate biscuit or two and a bag of crisps. Other boxes contained well-filled sandwiches and fruit. Tomato sauce sandwiches were rare but sometimes were enjoyed! Over the years I looked I found the foods improved in quality almost everywhere. Dinner helpers and teachers are most diligent in checking the contents of boxes and letting the head know of any concern.

Taking up the matter of food with a parent is a delicate business but often a class teacher who knows the family well can advise a parent or guardian without offence. Healthy eating must be tackled through lessons and by the example of tuck shops that do not run counter to the principles of good health education. (They tend to sell unhealthy food (sweets and crisps) because these make more money for school funds.)

I shall deal with the health implications of diet in Chapter 11.

Critical periods and school

The primary years fit into the criteria applied earlier to critical times (see Chapter 1). The rates of growth are steady, and unspectacular except for the small mid-childhood spurt. The brain seems to complete its growth in *weight* when a child is aged about 8.

Language

Those gross changes in height and weight are but a meagre clue to internal brain development, as I have continually stressed, and this period of life contains perhaps the classical case of a critical period – the acquisition and organisation of language. The period is a long one, extending between the ages of approximately 2 and 12 years. During the early part of this period the organisation of language may be easily modified in almost any direction – that is, any language may become the native language of an individual who is adopted from one culture into another at an early age. Towards the end of the period, though, it becomes more and more difficult (although not impossible) to learn a second language. By the age of 13 or so, a second language can only be learned with a non-native accent.

There have been a number of 'tests' of the critical time for language development over the years. An early one is the story of the Wild Boy of Aveyron who was captured in the forest when he was about 11 or 12 in 1799. He was a child without language and was at first thought to be deaf, since he showed very little reaction to quite loud sounds. Then it was realised that in fact his hearing was acute but that he only paid attention to sounds which meant something to him, like the noise of cracking walnuts, a food which he liked. His speech had not developed because nothing in the environment had stimulated its development.

A less bizarre but cruel 'test' is provided by the remarkable story of Genie. From the age of twenty months until her admission to hospital at about 14, Genie suffered terrible deprivation – isolated in a small, closed room, tied to a potty chair where she remained all the time, sometimes all night. No one spoke to her. She was a prisoner with no language for the 11 crucial years between 2 and puberty. Now, as a result of exposure to speech, she can speak like a 2- or 3-year-old but understands much more. Her progress is slow and uncertain and like the bird who learns to sing early at the right time but whose song is impaired at the wrong one, Genie will never acquire normal speech.

The critical period for language acquisition can be more precisely defined by the evidence from children who have suffered brain damage from various accidents. Before the age of twenty months, language development may be delayed in some cases, but otherwise there is no deficiency. This is prior to the age when language appears, and obviously the organisation process has not yet begun. From 21 to 36 months, damage has the effect of destroying all language abilities, which then reappear as they did in the beginning. From 3 to 10 years, accident or disease may prevent speech but eventually there is complete recovery except for some effects on reading and writing. After about age 10, changes produced by the damage are irreversible.

The evidence concerning the organisation of language acquisition is similar in form to that of attachment behaviour spoken of in Chapter 1 – namely, that there is an early period of very rapid development (pre-school) which then falls off to a lower rate but never goes down to zero.

Such compelling evidence demands greater attention to teaching power, quality and general resources at the primary level. The critical, overarching time from the nursery years right up to puberty must not be wasted; yet although basic skills work in English and mathematics is 'satisfactory or better' the picture deteriorates when more advanced language and mathematical skills and applications are considered.

Children's language, of course, is shaped by their lives at home and at school, not only speech but reading and writing and the love of story and poetry. They do not learn to speak, read or write once and for all and are forever needing help at ascending levels of difficulty and in widening fields of learning. On talking and listening many teachers at this level do not give children time to reflect and think and do not know when to hold back or intervene to prevent stagnation. Many questions asked by teachers require a single answer and give no encouragement to children to speculate or predict.

One point of detail about vocabulary and critical times is interesting and a possible useful confirmation of practice. Should one try to enlarge a child's vocabulary when he is just beginning to learn words? The answer is possibly that undue emphasis on individual words may baulk sentence learning and the acquiring of skills in rapid, uninterrupted speech. Emphasis is better placed on learning organised language rather than its isolated parts, and with this most teachers will agree.

Less direct, but still compelling, evidence of the critical times of the primary years is the push towards linguistic and spatial accomplishments at about aged 7 and 8 during the mid-growth spurt. At about 8, although children have poor staying power and tend to 'flit', they have developed active intellectual curiosity.

The majority of children at about 8 will leap ahead in reading and will enjoy books, although some will need to be heard to read daily. Most will write well, but some will produce ill-written, meagre stories and descriptions which to some extent reflect their lives and what is expected of them at school and given to them as mental fuel.

Mathematics and science

In the last chapter I said that the brain structure of girls and boys is slightly different, placing the girls ahead in speech at 4 or 5. It is necessary to explain this briefly by referring to the brain hemispheres.

Although the left and right hemispheres are constructed identically, they have different superiorities. The left hemisphere is usually associated with language, speech and logic. Indeed, the cells in the left side of the brain may be a mapping system for the storage, placing and understanding of words.

The right hemisphere is responsible for a collection of functions: recognising and remembering patterns such as faces and sounds like music. It helps with complex spatial tasks like dressing, finding our way about, or reading a map. It is rather like a spatial mapping system.

But the left and right halves work together as an integrated system to ensure unity of mental activity and behaviour and are connected by a huge nerve strap.

Brain circuitry in girls and boys is very slightly different and this may have a bearing on language development and probably on the early development of mathematical and scientific abilities. The speech areas in the left hemisphere are, as mentioned in the last chapter, slightly more advanced by about two months in girls of 4 or 5 than in boys of the same age. Parallel with this the speech organs of girls are more advanced – on average they talk earlier than boys. In boys, on the other hand, the right hemisphere is more developed and their capacity for spatial work with patterns and shapes is better – even from age 2. Boys also excel in the exploration of things. Cultural influences must be considerable, but there must be inherited components.

Exploring and experimenting are both likely to have a bearing on learning mathematics and science, *which in the very early stages are not learned through talk but by experimenting and playing under skilled guidance with water, sand, shapes and so on*. Given time, boys can catch up on language, but girls may not catch up so easily on play experiences that involve mathematical and scientific ideas. At pre-school and primary school more numerical, experimental and spatial activities for girls should be planned so that they can learn much more through experiment, as well as through talk.

Whatever factors cause the differences in mathematical ability in boys and girls they are in operation by the time children are in the primary school. So early experience of number relationships by *doing* is especially important for girls.

Pattern and order

I remarked in the last chapter that pre-school children begin to look for patterns in the environment to explain their world. This suggests that somehow the brain is not haphazard in scanning the world but searches for order and it even guesses and uses clues to decide what the order might be. It might do this by looking for linking features or 'clues' to make sense of an object such as a chair – four vertical lines and a horizontal one. The linking feature appear to give clues to build up the picture just as when one makes a jigsaw puzzle one looks for clues of blue sky or brickwork in order to narrow the search for matching pieces.

The brain does not have in it cells to identify particular things like an arm or face or house; rather, it uses general features in its analyses: colour, depth, edges, corners and so on. We do not know yet that the human brain has in it cells that identify these features but animals certainly have specific nerve cells in the visual cortex which respond electrically – that is, 'fire' – to stimuli from a whole range of shapes: slits, lines, corner shapes, colour and movement. It may be that we have such cells in our visual cortex, the part of the brain responsible for vision. How these primitive patterns of visual impressions unite to form fully integrated images such as a person or a chair is a mystery.

The business of searching for pattern to explain the world seems to be inborn, but as one grows up it must be immensely modified by cultural influences. Left to himself a child, as remarked on earlier, will seldom tire of making all-over patterns. Children love regularity, symmetry and continuity of line, rather as they like and respond to rhythm in music.

Teachers should strengthen this natural tendency of children to look for pattern through most subjects taught – maths, science, art and craft, spelling and handwriting, to name a few. For example, 6- and 7-year-olds have word books to help them to spell words they are using in stories. The teacher writes the word in the book. But to help plant the word in the visual memory the child should follow a 'look, cover, write, check' routine: look at the word first, cover it up, write it out from memory and then check that it is correct. Dr Margaret Peters,[6] whose idea this is, suggests this way because the secret of learning to spell is linked to the ability of the brain to absorb letter patterns.

Sorting equipment – matching clothes to the size of dolls, for example – helps establish the idea of one-to-one correspondence and ordering by size.

Looking for patterns is at the heart of science. Children

make observations and carry out experiments at school; these give information which is then scrutinised for possible patterns and relationships. Ten-year-olds measure their height, skin area and size of feet, collect a lot of data and test out whether the tallest people have the largest feet. Similarly, older junior children finding out about the easiest way to pull a nail out of a piece of wood will discover by observation and experiment – and discussion – the value of a pivot, and the function of a lever and the importance of the length of its arms.

In handwriting, mentioned in the last chapter, children in the infant school soon see that the patterns of some letters are joined to others (e.g. by a horizontal stroke and some by a diagonal one) and come to recognise that a word is a complete piece of pattern. Many schools neglect the steady practice of pattern and letter formation and later work in all areas is adversely affected by this lack of groundwork. It might be added that handwriting is the visible mark on paper of hand *movement* and one which involves the whole body. The basic motor movement once taught in the reception class and laid down in nerve pathways is difficult to alter. To ignore movement errors will lead to serious writing problems later which are hard to eradicate.

This point and others made about pattern and order and learning complex skills like handwriting emphasise the importance of the quality of early experience in nursery and primary schools. Once through the critical times from birth to puberty, the capacity for rapid learning and forming a host of good habits and skills is over.

Learning off by heart

Finally, some of the most telling evidence that these years are critical comes from what we remember of them in later life. People of 80 can still remember the smell of the school room, tables, poems learned, and bits of the Bible. Early habits, and skills and things learned 'by heart' during the nursery and primary years, as indicated earlier, are deeply ingrained in nerve pathways; they involve mechanisms of extreme complexity at levels ranging from simple nerve pathways to the higher levels of the brain. Listen to the most eminent person who has had a 'local' start, and happily traces of dialect stick. Handwriting is another miracle of constancy and a source of wonder and usefulness to our bank manager.

Other important skills and habits have the same basis: swimming, riding a bike, walking, eating, throwing, playing a game or an instrument, drawing and painting. Once learned these skills are not strictly conscious and come naturally.

Though there have been many gains in schooling, one of the losses that I noted in almost 30 years as HMI was learning off by heart – nursery rhymes, tables, poems, hymns, and much else. I remember my father, who was born in 1900, reciting, for pleasure and sometimes solace, poems from *The Golden Treasury* and pieces of the Bible that he had learned before he was 10 or 11. And I, at school in the 1930s, along with many of my contemporaries, can remember poems, tables, spelling props – 'i' before 'e' except after 'c' – and can still sing a verse or two of a childhood hymn without having to look down at the page. Those hymns, especially Mrs Alexander's 'There is a green hill far away' and 'All things bright and beautiful', come back easily and were learned early.

It is a pity that learning off by heart is neglected at this time by home and school when what is learned is likely to remain impressed on the nervous system: fine lines of poetry, nursery rhymes, number jingles, the hymns of John Milton, Charles Wesley, George Herbert and, especially in infancy, those of Mrs Alexander, and much else. It is true, of course, that what is learned early on will not always be understood, but it will come later to give pleasure and even solace in times of need.

In a general sense, carefully planned, systematic and structural work which takes place in an orderly and supportive climate is necessary to meet the wide range of intellectual and imaginative powers of children. Each child, however meagre his or her abilities, needs hope and confidence. Co-operation with parents strengthens the aims and work of a school. If all this happens, the critical phase, and its impact on the growth and development of the brain, will have been well used. As the Introduction to this book points out, many thousands of children get a raw deal at school. Many schools struggle against the indifference or the excessive demands of parents; against narrow-minded governors; against a hard core of pupils who disrupt the life and work of the school to consume the time and energy of head and staff.

What is learned during the receptive primary years will never be so easily acquired again and much will remain for life. If this potentially fertile time is made barren by poor teaching and inadequate spending on education (as is happening now), millions of children will have lost out.

References

1 *Primary Education* (HMSO, 1959).
2 M. A. Holliday, 'Body composition and energy needs during growth', in F. Falkner and J. M. Tanner (eds), *Human Growth* (Plenum Press, 1986).
3 J. P. Scott, 'Critical periods in organisational processes', in F. Falkner and J. M. Tanner (eds), *Human Growth* (Plenum Press, 1986).
4 DHSS, *The Diets of British School Children* (HMSO, 1989).
5 Ministry of Agriculture, Fisheries and Food, *Manual of Nutrition* (HMSO, 1985).
6 Margaret Peters, *Spelling: Caught or Taught* (Routledge, 1967).

Chapter 8

PUBERTY

Puberty describes the changes that happen in the growing boy or girl as the reproductive organs change from the infantile to the adult stage. Most of the organs and structures of the body are involved and puberty is not complete until the individual can conceive and successfully bring up children. The changes of puberty vary from individual to individual in their time of onset and in the length of time to reach completion.

The obvious manifestations of puberty are growth in height and changes in shape – wider hips in the girl, shoulders in the boy. They conceal other developments in the reproductive organs, changes in body composition and development of the heart and lungs, all leading, especially in boys, to an increase in strength and powers of endurance (see Photographs 4, 5 and 6).

In girls the growth spurt starts on average about 10 and begins to increase in rate at about 10½ to reach its maximum velocity at around 12.[1] Though the peak velocity in growth in height varies from one child to the next it is on average about 9 cm/year for girls. For about a year, that is six months either side of the peak growth rate, the average speed of growth is about 8.5 cm/year. For boys growth rate starts to rise at about 12½, peak velocity is about 14 at around 10 cm/year, and 9.5 cm/year for the year surrounding the peak. Thus, for about a year the rate of growth is nearly twice the velocity of that occurring just before puberty (around 5 cm/year). These gross changes in speed of growth fit the criteria of a critical period of development, though what is happening to the brain then is unknown. As far as is known it does not accelerate in growth at puberty but, as remarked earlier, size is a poor measure of efficiency. Patterns of nerve connectivity are more important and as yet there are only the most primitive ways of measuring them.

Photograph 4 Secondary boys aged 12/13. A group on the verge of puberty – the time at which the misleading nature of chronological age is seen most clearly because of the immense variation in the rate of normal physical development. This photograph shows a range of body build, but note the length of leg. At this time most boys will be growing out of their trousers. A year later they will be growing out of their jackets as their trunk lengthens. Note the relatively large hands and feet (alarming to some girls), but by the time the growth spurt is over hands and feet will be smaller in proportion to arms, legs and height.

Growth of nearly all skeletal dimensions takes place at puberty. There is a greater increase in length of trunk than in length of leg and so the proportion of total height due to the trunk rises during adolescence.

The growth spurt also begins at different times in different parts of the body. The peak growth rate in leg length happens six months before that for the trunk so boys have trousers at half-mast and grow out of them before they grow out of their coats. The foot has its peak growth rate earliest of all and attains adult size, to the horror of girls who think their feet will continue to grow, long before any other region except perhaps the head. Most of the facial dimensions reach maximum velocity a few months after peak height velocity and are more pronounced in boys than in girls. The shape of a boy's face, jaw and neck changes, the larynx develops and

Photograph 5 Secondary boys aged 14/15. Note increase in limb muscle and in shape of jaw, now more angular than in the boys in Photograph 4, a development which makes the chin more pointed. Facial muscles also develop, making the face less chubby than in earlier photographs.

the voice deepens. Sometimes a girl's face hardly changes. Girls have a particularly large spurt in hip width during adolescence. Shoulder-width spurt is marked in boys.

Boys begin their height spurt two years later than girls. At this time they are about 9 cm taller than girls are when they begin their height spurt at about 12. The sex difference in *adult* height is about 13 cm. This is roughly divided as follows: at 12 when girls start their height spurt, boys are 2 cm taller;

Photograph 6 At about 12, on average, girls reach their maximum velocity in growth but note the normal range of heights in this class. Compare with Photograph 4 and note the relatively longer legs of the boys in relation to their trunk, and the greater hip width and relatively fatter limbs of the girls. See text for other details.

the delay in the boys' spurt accounts for a further 7 cm difference, and the boys' spurt itself is some 4 cm greater than the girls'. The longer period of pre-adolescent growth in boys accounts for men's longer legs in relation to their trunk because, as remarked above, legs grow faster than the trunk just before adolescence.

Internally, peak growth rate in heart and lungs coincides with the peak of the height growth spurt in both sexes. Muscular growth in the limbs in boys is maximal at about the same time as the peak velocity in height. Fat accumulation drops in rate. In fact, boys become thinner, particularly in the limbs but not in the trunk, during adolescence. Girls continue to become fatter but at a slower rate during the growth spurt than before or after it.

The first sign of puberty in a girl is usually the enlargement of the breast bud with some appearance of pubic hair. This usually happens about 11 on average in the UK but may range from 8–13. In advanced girls the breasts may be fully mature by 12 but in others the process is not completed before 19. Adult distribution of pubic hair is usually attained between 12 and 17. In most boys full adult hair is seldom reached until the mid-20s. Hair first appears just after 12 but does not grow rapidly until the growth spurt at 14.[1]

Although the peak of the growth spurt happens earlier in girls than in boys by about two years, other aspects of sexual development do not take place much later in boys than girls. Boys' reproductive organs start to develop about the same time as breasts in girls and complete sexual maturity is reached about the same average age in both sexes. Girls' looks at puberty – bigger than boys, with obvious breast development – make 11- and 12-year-old boys look immature. But in boys the early development of the reproductive organs is concealed by clothes and the obvious changes – the shooting up in height, deepening of the voice, and the development of facial hair – do not happen until the reproductive organs are nearly mature. Menarche is usually a late event in puberty and it is very rare for a girl to menstruate before she has passed her peak height spurt.

Underlying the growth process, and indeed the start of puberty, is the control of hormones. Without them normal growth and development will not occur nor will the normal changes of the progression from child to adult.[2] The hormonal control of growth and development in children is becoming well understood now. Puberty is started by the release of a hormone by nerve cells in the hypothalamus at the base of the brain. This in turn causes other hormones to be secreted in larger quantities from the ovaries or testes and the adrenal glands. These hormones are the immediate causes of the changes of puberty – the growth spurt, changes in body fat/ muscle ratio, and the appearance of the secondary sexual characteristic: breaking of voice, axillary and facial hair.

As with the instruments of an orchestra, no hormone is more important than another in the process of growth and adolescence, and a deficiency of any will lead to impaired growth.

PE and games

It cannot be stressed too strongly that there is enormous and quite normal variation in the timing of these changes at puberty. A boy who has had his growth spurt early has the advantage of size and strength in the playground, on the sports-field, and in the peer group. They are but temporary assets and his smaller fellows will generally catch him up. The late maturers sometimes wonder whether they will ever grow up, or will they be forever weedy and bottom dog. They need reassurance that they will not always be smaller and weaker than their peers.[3]

In girls, the early developer, conscious of her developing breasts, may slouch and find the public conditions of showers after games or PE an agony that needs great understanding from adults. The girl who slouches and wears a shapeless cardigan to hide her growing breasts appears clumsy to the beholder. The later maturer may have her problems too, wondering privately whether she will ever grow up into a sexually normal adult.

In these respects and others it is most important that teachers should discuss the normality of human variation at this time, and, for example, should thus reassure a girl if one of her breasts enlarges before the other or a boy who is embarrassed by the temporary enlargement of his breasts. Time will put these worries right but they are hard to bear at the time. Indeed, if children are not taught about the wide variation in normal growth and development (and not enough are) they perceive such variance as abnormal – in some cases, to the detriment of their psychological development.

Children at this age require, but now rarely get, a variety of opportunities to match their physical development. Lack of money and equipment, and competition for precious time between the subjects of the National Curriculum often relegate physical education to a lowly position. Team games, gymnastics, athletics, swimming, outdoor pursuits and expressive movement and dance provide the variety important at this age. It is not an easy age and both sexes have plenty of individuals who prefer to sit about talking in the warm and who need prodding into activity. Team games are perhaps given too much emphasis at this age (11–15). These games tend to be enjoyed by rapidly maturing boys who have the skill, vigour and agility, but, with some exceptions, the rapidly maturing girl seems to lose enthusiasm for team games. Perhaps more in the way of movement and dance would be suitable for girls.

Diet

In Chapter 7 I mentioned the main foods eaten by 10-year-olds. They are broadly similar to those eaten by 14-year-olds but I want to add a detail or two.

Parents and teachers know that snacking and eating fast foods and take-aways are common among teenagers, who are more influenced by peer and other social pressure than by nutritional knowledge. It would be odd indeed if they were too bothered by health and diet. The 14-year-old collecting his/her burger, chips, doughnut and fizzy drink after a lesson on balanced diet is a commonplace observation. Indeed, chips form 11 per cent of the energy intake of 14-year-olds followed by milk at between 9 and 10 per cent. These older children eat half their chips at school dinners.[4]

Some older children, especially girls, often eat out during the lunch hour at cafés and choose meals low in many nutrients, particularly iron, protein and calcium. The nutritional quality of the daily diets of these older girls in particular is lower than in any other group of girls who have lunch at home or school or bring a packed lunch. At least 5 per cent of them are dieting to lose weight and are preoccupied with their body image. They tend to cut out milk, bread, cereals and potatoes as 'fattening' foods. Consequently, many do not achieve the RDA for calcium, iron or riboflavin. *The Diets of British School Children*[4] shows that almost 60 per cent of 14–15-year-old girls eat too little calcium.

Despite this gloom, children of this age group are on average taller and heavier than ever before. Boys of 14/15 are about 167 cm tall and girls 161 cm, compared with the standards of 164 and 161 cm. Weights for boys of this age are on average

56 kg, girls 54 kg, compared with the standards of 52 and 53 kg respectively.

Children at puberty have large appetites and it is important that they have well-balanced meals and not too many snacks rich in fat, sugar or salt. Calorie intake is on average 2,500 for boys and about 2,000 for girls. This is 10 per cent lower than official recommendations and reflects a decrease in physical activity rather than an inadequate energy intake.

There is clearly a lot of room for improvement and I shall take up the health implications of schoolchildren's diet and other matters in Chapter 11.

Critical periods and school

The increased rate of growth at puberty is about the same as it was at 2 or 3: about 9–10 cm/year. The change to this velocity from the relative steady growth during the primary school years marks an especially critical time. Details of brain development are unknown, but the plasticity of its nerve networks to the effect of hormones and to the environment cannot be discounted.

While nothing is known about changes in brain circuitry at this time, it is known that during the later primary years the development of a child's thinking is concerned with ordering, classifying, and rearranging *things*, either in front of him (sticks, apples, counters or whatever) or in the 'mind's eye', though a small proportion will need the solid objects in front of their eye for long after 10 or 11. Piaget called this the period of 'concrete operations'. By 'concrete' he meant *thinking* about doing things with physical objects. By 'operations' he meant actions (not of body but of mind) such as the mental groupings mentioned above. For example, if a child of 8 is asked the question, 'Edith is fairer than Susan. Edith is darker than Lily. Who is darkest?', most cannot solve it in their heads but if they were asked to arrange three actual dolls in serial order the task would be easy. Many 11-year-olds would solve it in their heads because they are now at the stage of concrete operations.

These developments in thinking go on during the primary years described earlier. During puberty there is a change of crucial importance in thinking, but like all developmental processes its timing varies from individual to individual. The subject matter a boy or girl can now deal with may be *ideas and events outside previous experience*; the hallmark is the ability to think logically. Looked at in quite another way, the brain is freed from concern only with immediate concrete details and enabled to use what has been learned in new ways; for example, to predict what might happen given a certain set of facts. To be able to forecast is the essence of man's success and would be strongly preserved in evolution. Piaget called this the period of 'formal operations'; 'formal' because *ideas* can now be manipulated. If a child of 13 can make a stab at the question 'Why does the size of penguins increase the nearer one gets to the South Pole?', using his knowledge of surface area to volume ratio in a *new situation*, he is moving into the formal operational stage of thinking.

A few children arrive early at this stage of thinking at 11 or 12, most much later at 14 or 15; some never reach it fully. I believe that for most of us the critical period during puberty enhances the development of formal thinking whose base is physically in brain structures that we do not yet understand. It certainly is a capacity that would have helped man to survive in the long past.

Of course, a cut-and-dried account like this bears little relationship to the reality before a teacher in his class of 13- or 14-year-olds or indeed to himself. At times he himself will use a concrete method of thinking, using objects in his mind to visualise a solution – particularly in the face of an unfamiliar problem. To project to a 'higher', 'formal' level of thinking he may particularise from concrete examples in his mind's eye before moving to an abstract idea.

To develop this ability it is necessary to provide the stimulus in lessons and to have the resources. Crudely, just as the retina requires light to develop properly, the brain needs stimulus to develop and release its powers. Some children are fortunate. Many are not. For example, the ability to make a tentative hypothesis on the basis of preliminary enquiries and to then design an experiment or make observations to test it is at the heart of science and of formal thinking. But at least one-quarter of all science teaching at the secondary level is unsatisfactory, though where standards are highest pupils 'design their own experiments, draw their own conclusions and evaluate their own work'.[5]

Most subjects foster this mental gift, but variations in standards of work in mathematics, science, English and technology, all of which will contribute, are a national cause of concern. Action by government, local authorities and teachers themselves is needed rapidly to remedy this situation or potential will go to waste.

The slow and the gifted

Adolescence is, as indicated above, probably one of the most formative and crucial periods of the entire life-span in developing the ability to think. As such, the environment needs to provide a good ethos: guidance, stimulus, the right level of expectation, and exemplars of suitable behaviour from parents and teachers.

Organisation of the curriculum, its content, the way it is modified to meet individual needs, and its methods should provide genuine 'access' and equality for different groups of pupils: boys and girls, minority ethnic groups, the academically poor and the gifted among them. At this time when the body is growing fast the influences of school and home will have a powerful effect on the brain's nerve networks and learning processes.

IQ

This section of the book says a little about the use of this critical time by the slow and the gifted and also about single-sex and co-educational schools, but I need to say something first about IQ, which is pertinent to the slow and the gifted especially.

The IQ test provides a teacher with crucial information on which to base his teaching methods, his grouping of children by ability and, particularly important, his expectations for the pupil. This test, to be sure, says nothing of the fine grain of the mind. It is also important to stress that children should be given IQ tests periodically to provide a picture of differential mental development and to overcome anxieties about being graded on a single test. Emotional upset, anxiety, insufficient interest in school work, ill-health, poor sight and slight deafness can all affect the result of a test.

IQ tests are a reasonable measure of an important human attribute – intelligence: the ability to grasp the essentials of a situation and respond appropriately to them. It is important to remember that intelligent activity can be affected by mood, aspiration, and so on. Thus lack of interest in school work will lower 'functional intelligence'. Low expectations will breed low standards of attainment. Put crudely, thinking and feeling are hard to separate.

Cyril Burt[6] defined intelligence as: 'innate, general, cognitive ability'; innate because it is inborn, general because it enters into every form of mental ability, and cognitive because it is an intellectual quality: that is it involves knowing rather than feeling. But there are some obvious weaknesses in the restricted definition.

There are brilliant musicians and gifted painters with an IQ of about 90, and many children whose minds a teacher may envy but who have moderate IQs and yet turn out to have flair in experimental work or literature. While IQ score is an important piece of information about a child it needs to be used in conjunction with observation. The opinion of a careful, observant teacher provides the matrix in which to set IQ.

Some of the most difficult boys and girls (often in the rung above the very slowest and with modest IQs) are at times reflective, idealistic and thoughtful, marking another kind of mental development characteristic of this age.

Nevertheless, the boy or girl in this group often has difficulty with reading, writing and mathematics. Such children are not in the main unintelligent. Because of a disadvantaged background they can start off school at 5 with an IQ score some 25 points below that of their peers who have had the advantage of stories on mother's knee, books and conversation and a keen interest taken in their school programme by parents. They very often have difficulty in realising the significance of what they are asked to learn. They are often antagonistic to school and school authority, so there attendance record is often poor. Apathy and indifference can mark them out.

Cheeringly enough, that boy or girl who possesses some or all of the above characteristics has often demonstrated his or her potential in some other of the following ways.

He or she is often able to cope with a very difficult environment. Indeed, a boy or girl who is capable of surviving in a slum environment or on a bleak housing estate must have considerable adaptability. They are often able to concentrate for long periods of time when working at things of interest to them – the complexities of car engines or dressmaking. They can show considerable insight into human behaviour and can often show more maturity and ability to function in various social situations, for example at camp, than many good A-level students. Usually they are able to talk about something meaningful to them with enthusiasm and interest even though they cannot write much about it.

Poor and shoddy teaching

These less able pupils, according to official reports, 'are much more likely to experience the poor and shoddy than the more able – a worrying persistent feature of English education – at all levels'.[5] Consequently, for many boys and girls this especially critical time is wasted.

By 'shoddy' I mean, among many other things, lessons which fail to start on time. This is sometimes the fault of the teacher, sometimes due to pupils arriving late. The pace of lessons is often too slow so that the work is boring and unprogressive with a class gaining little sense of achievement. Consequently the work is held in low regard (significance has been mentioned above). Shoddy teaching sometimes consists of lessons lacking a clear introduction of their purpose (important where attendance is intermittent), together with a review of previous work, so that pupils are vague about the significance of what they are to be taught. There is often too little involvement of the teacher and class in discussion and too much reliance on the delivery of instructions and information by worksheets. Sometimes diagnosis of a particular difficulty a class encounters is poor and the teacher tends to counter failure with a generally lower demand by, for example, asking pupils to draw and colour a simple picture instead of writing. Lack of order may allow pupils to come and go (in a laboratory, for example) without permission, with consequent dangers. Homework is set irregularly, sometimes impeded by a lack of books or sets of books kept back in school. Marking is often superficial and comments, when made, are vague and give poor advice for improvement and so on.

Nevertheless some pupils, so-called 'failures', eventually learn to master complex skills in industry, commerce and building, or pass tough driving tests to become drivers of heavy goods vehicles. Experienced heads say candidly that they were wrong about certain boys and girls.

There is, of course, a proportion who will end up in dead-end jobs or will be unemployed. It is these in particular who lack that most powerful of all educational forces – parental aspiration – and often do not have what an inspector described in his reports over a century ago as 'that recognition which our natures crave for and acknowledge with a renewed endeavour'.

Gifted children

Going to the other extreme of giftedness, other but rather different problems exist. Broadly speaking, gifted children may be thought of as children of superior all-round intellectual ability, confirmed where possible by reliable IQ tests giving an IQ of 130 or more, *or* those of lower IQ who are outstanding in particular academic areas or in music, sport, dance and art. These are rough criteria and identifying the gifted is not always easy. What is clear, as mentioned a moment ago, is that it is the teacher who is in the front line when it comes to identification. In most schools identification is a hit-and-miss affair with the initiative coming mainly from individual teachers.

This book is concerned with critical times of development and not with the details of giftedness or talent, but if school time passes without giftedness being spotted and encouraged the development of talent may be baulked.

One obstacle is the common irrational distrust of cleverness ('too clever by half'), which appears as a threat to the self-esteem of the less clever and can provoke disapproving or derisory comments from them – twitting and ridicule. Such an attitude among adults (including teachers) is soon caught by children, and the clever child against whom it is directed quickly learns to take avoiding action and conceals his ability.

Another obstacle is that giftedness is more obvious in some subjects than in others. In the active subjects like PE, music, art and drama, outstanding ability is more easily observable. In physics (electronics) it is a boy or girl who has sheer technical skill who is more easily spotted; in biology, the keen naturalist with a sharp eye. Specialist teachers will recognise such children but perhaps some gifted all-rounders are missed because of poor consultation between teachers.

Third, experience built up by a school needs to be used to improve parental backing of gifted pupils. A gifted child may be doubly handicapped if the school is failing him and if his home is not interested and fails to understand his ability.

Fourth, classrooms can inhibit talent instead of encouraging it. The teacher may treat unusual questions either as ridiculous or as a nuisance, even though they are both genuine and intelligent. True, questions that are ill-timed and full of opportunities for discussion raise problems that cannot be adequately explained at the time. Consequently they may be seen as unwelcome interruptions, even as disruptive. An unduly formal classroom, with many rules and prescriptions, can be particularly restrictive for a gifted child.

Enhancing giftedness

Two situations are necessary to enhance the potential of the gifted during school time whether it be primary or secondary school. First, for the child to meet with the right individual teacher. If the past history of famous men and women is looked at, many teachers have provided the right environment for a gifted child.

At the secondary level in particular there needs to be a sufficient supply of teachers who are not simply graduates in particular subjects but who are committed to the intricacies and subtleties of these subjects for their own sakes – teachers who actually love mathematics or physics or French or history and who can therefore delight in a pupil who is also going to love the same thing.

Second, the presence of a few other children of similar giftedness in a group. There need not be many, but 'critical mass' is important. The occasional withdrawal of individual pupils from a class for the purpose of working with a small number of like-minded pupils is a particularly useful form of provision. Staffing implications, of course, arise.

I have mentioned IQ but, as I have implied, it is never the sole forecaster of success: persistence and imagination are powerful attributes. Indeed most (boys) who return to school driving Bentleys are not those who achieved three As at A-level; they have other qualities, often of character. The 'gifted' commonly discussed are often the future professionals – scientists, doctors, engineers, architects – and a distinction between the 'gifted' and the 'clever' is necessary. The former have *flair*. The clever are often pedestrian. They have a high IQ but may be devoid of imagination and persistence and may (and sometimes do) simply fizzle out.

I have mentioned the slow, the clever, and the gifted as part of the spectrum of ability that appears in classes; there is also the genius. Nothing will stop the *genius* who creates his or her own environment. Witness the instance of Dickens, who achieved immortality despite starting his working life in a blacking factory, and D. H. Lawrence, Ernie Bevin, or Charlie Chaplin, who all rose from poor circumstances. But for the majority of pupils – gifted, slow, and middle range – the environment is especially crucial in the critical time of adolescence in particular. It is questionable whether that quality of environment exists now in many maintained schools as cuts bite and teacher morale falls.

Single-sex or co-educational schools

One perennial question is whether single-sex or co-educational schools at the secondary stage are better for fostering character and academic ability. At a time when physical, intellectual and emotional development are proceeding fast the span of time between about 11 and 16 is critical and needs to be well used, and answers to the questions are needed.

In making a choice (if this is possible) between a mixed or single-sex school the ability and the personality of the boy or girl need careful consideration, as does the breadth of experience offered by the school in addition to the range of its academic work. These suggestions apply to both state and independent schools. Most parents will not have a choice, but in some cities single-sex schools do exist so some choice is possible. In practice most children go to the nearest school, which in nine cases out of ten will be mixed.

Mixed schools at the secondary stage are a natural extension of the family and the primary school. They allow (from age 5) for the development of some understanding of the characters of the opposite sex and some experience of relationships with them. With the majority they succeed well, but there are gains and losses. One gain (relationships and understanding of the opposite sex) has been noted. In subtle ways, however, the balance is weighted to the boys' benefit. Girls tend to civilise the boys just as female influence in a family raises standards of manners, hygiene and grace. Academically girls lose out, particularly in the physical sciences and in technology, where they are not as confident in experimental work as the boys. Boys are more likely to get the use of computers and other science equipment. Girls are quieter in class, not asking questions or venturing opinions, and thus boys get more attention. Girls are more afraid of making fools of themselves in front of the boys, who bother less and are not afraid to express an opinion. Perhaps, also, the characters of the girls do not flourish quite as well in a mixed as in a single-sex school. For the reasons give above some mixed schools use single-sex groups for particular purposes: science lessons, for example. The usefulness of this arrangement in a mixed school has not been adequately established.

Brain circuitry supports the notion of common abilities between the sexes and is broadly similar in boys and girls. It seems from this brain evidence that the potentiality for doing all but the tiniest fraction of jobs appears to exist in both sexes. This is why all pupils should receive a broad and balanced education. There are slight *average* differences explained in Chapter 7 in spatial and linguistic abilities between boys and girls. The greatest difference, however, is in exploratory behaviour, in which boys excel from an early age and which helps boys to embark on new things – practical work, discussion, and a whole variety of tasks – with less trepidation than girls.

I have made some suggestions about choice a moment ago but if there is choice then perhaps the most important considered for a *girl* is her character (most boys will survive in a mixed school). While the extrovert will probably flourish in a mixed school there are some introverted, shy girls who might do better in a single-sex school; but on the whole co-education for the large majority of boys and girls is successful. Boarding schools in particular exaggerate the need for a girl's character to be extroverted, more so if girls are taken into a sixth form only and if the ratio of girls to boys is low throughout the school as it is in some independent schools.

Policies of equal opportunity which give genuine access to a broad curriculum, modified to meet individual needs, are of central importance. Underlying them should be the knowledge that critical periods exist, with that of puberty being vital.

References

1 W. A. Marshall and J. M. Tanner, 'Puberty' in F. Falkner and J. M. Tanner (eds), *Human Growth* (Plenum Press, 1986).
2 M. A. Preece, 'Pre-pubertal and pubertal endocrinology' in F. Falkner and J. M. Tanner (eds), *Human Growth* (Plenum Press, 1986).
3 J. M. Tanner, *Education and Physical Growth* (University of London Press, 1978).
4 DHSS, *The Diets of British School Children* (HMSO, 1989).
5 DES, *Standards in Education*, 1988–89 (HMSO, 1990).
6 Cyril Burt, *Mental and Scholastic Tests* (Staples, 1962).

Chapter 9

GROWTH AND INTELLIGENCE

Some curious and interesting facts link growth with intelligence in an amusing way. Gifted children are usually big and strong and not, as expected, studious weeds. Taller women tend to move to more skilled jobs than smaller ones. Migrants are taller and more intelligent than those who stay at home. Boys who go to Oxford from state schools are taller than the average at their school and taller than boys from public schools. Physically large children score higher in IQ tests than small ones from the age of 6 onwards.[1] Then, early maturing children score higher in IQ tests than later maturing children and when they have finished growing some of the height–IQ difference persists into adulthood.

'Intelligence', as implied in the last chapter, is a much abused concept and raises heat in discussion because people mind about brains even more than looks. Intelligence is quite easily recognised when it is seen in action, but though I use it here as a kind of shorthand it is made up of multiple components and qualities which sometimes surprise – in particular when a child thought slow lifts a veil to show insight or specific talent. Classification by any single criterion can be misleading with regard to abilities and can cause a teacher to overlook a range of abilities or talents in other aspects of work.

Obviously not all tall people are intelligent nor short ones stupid, and differences only appear in large population samples. Nevertheless the height–IQ relationship, though tenuous, is persistent. The reasons for the association of tallness with higher IQ are not fully understood, but a mixture of genetic endowment and 'social environment' must be responsible.

Rising IQ

To examine this last statement more carefully one hard example is important: that of growth in height, in head size, and in intelligence over the last 50 years. Richard Lynn,[2] whose thesis that nutrition improvements explain all three, gives some remarkable evidence to show that the height of children and young adults in relatively rich countries like the UK has risen by 7–8 cm in the last 50 years. Head circumference of infants has increased by approximately 1.5–2 cm, and IQ by a remarkable 15 points.

There is no doubt that over 50 years ago, in the 1930s, poverty was widespread here and elsewhere. Numerous surveys have shown that nutrition then was sub-standard for large sections of the population, with less than half getting an adequate intake of vitamins and minerals. Old film of the 1930s shows thin men and hungry faces. But since the 1939–45 war rising living standards have enabled people to buy more nutritious foods. And children now, as we have seen, are taller and heavier than before.

Head size

Increased height correlates with increased head size, and this in turn strongly with brain size though brain size correlates rather weakly with intelligence. Common sense and observation also suggest that size is a poor measure of brain power – in any case small people have small heads. The average brain size of men and women differs also, that of women being smaller. This is not surprising because women are smaller, yet there is no difference between the sexes in intelligence. The position is as Dr Johnson put it when answering the question 'Which have the most brains, men or women?' 'Which man, Sir, which woman?' was his devastatingly accurate reply.

Better nutrition may be important in promoting the better brain 'connectivity' referred to in Chapter 1, and perhaps this, rather than brain size, may result in higher intelligence.

Twins, nutrition, and IQ

There are a few other good pieces of evidence which support Lynn's suggestions. Twins average some 4 to 7 IQ points lower than children born singly irrespective of home and back-ground, but their birth weights are lower than those of single-born children, indicating a poorer level of nutrition in the uterus.

More precisely, tests on one-egg twins with differing birth weights show that at about the age of 10 the lighter twin of each pair is about five IQ points lower than the heavier one. Conditions of growth in the uterus are quite likely to have caused the differences, with nutritional differences being a likely cause.

For teaching and learning, Lynn's nutrition theory implies that good nutrition will boost IQ. In the last twenty years considerable efforts have been expended in attempting to raise the intelligence of disadvantaged children through 'head-start' programmes. These have largely concentrated on stimulating pre-school children by various methods to boost ability levels measured by IQ tests or to develop linguistic ability. As expected, no magic solution exists to provide a once-and-for-all boost to performance no matter what the age of the child, and the gains made by children soon wash out.

Lynn suggests that better nutrition rather than stimulation is the more positive policy for tackling the problem of low intelligence. But no sound educational solution is based on a simple 'either/or' policy and a wider approach is necessary. Good nutrition certainly is important, but stimulation at home and school, stopping smoking in pregnancy, reducing stress – all these will help a child to achieve the genetic potential for height and IQ. Quality of family life and quality of school sum it up.

Schooling

Nutrition has certainly improved over the last 50 years but so has the quality of education. Both will have been major factors in unlocking and finding genetic potential for intelligence and other things. A century and a half ago school was practically non-existent and even thought to be dangerous by the 'selfish vulgar of the upper classes', as Matthew Arnold put it. Some of them believed, Arnold went on, that 'the less a poor man learned except his handicraft the better', and that

ıcate the poor was like putting the torch of knowledge
.o the hands of rick burners'.

In the middle of the last century, Joseph Kay, a Cambridge-
trained barrister, reported to ministers here on the social and
educational conditions of this and other European countries.
Kay, in his report, expressed the number of elementary school
pupils as a proportion of the total population in a number of
European states. The best was the Canton of Berne in Switzerland with one child in school for every 4.3 persons; Scotland
had one to eight. The very bottom was England and Wales
with one child in school for every fourteen people in the
country. Kay concluded his report[3] with these words:

> Here where the aristocracy is richer and more powerful than that
> of any other country in the world, the poor are more depressed,
> more pauperised, more numerous in comparison to other classes, more
> irreligious and very much worse educated than the poor of any other
> European country solely excepting Russia, Turkey, southern Italy,
> Portugal and Spain. Such a state of things cannot long continue.

What a bound from the attitudes described by Arnold and
Kay to those of the last 50 years! Although progress has been
uneven and its pace varied, there has been increasing attention to the worth of what is taught and to the quality of
children's learning. There has also been an ever-deepening
concern with children as individuals and with methods that
attempt to bring out the best for age, aptitude and ability.
Unfortunately we are now witnessing a downturn in standards
and attitudes compared with, say, 20 or 30 years ago when
people from the world over came to see our schools. Chapter
13 has more to say about school.

Inner-city children

The greatest concern in terms of nutrition, education, stress
and their effects on height and intelligence must be for those
children in inner cities. Some of these children will, to be sure,
come from happy homes and attend good schools, but averages
show worrying physical trends and schooling is often a cause
of concern.

A recent example from Liverpool[4] could be multiplied a thousand times. Body measurements made of over 500 primary children at two schools – one inner city, the other outer – showed that for each of twelve measurements made (including height, weight and head circumference), the inner-city children were on average smaller than outer-city children. It is likely also (though not commented on) that a high proportion of the inner-city children were slow learners. These particular children did not necessarily experience poor teaching, though children in many inner-city schools do. Teacher turnover (and poor attendance of pupils) is such that continuity in learning and high standards of achievement are virtually impossible. Some schools are so shabby that morale among staff and pupils is low. Repairs and, as Sir Alec Clegg, one-time CEO of the West Riding, once told me, 'a lick of paint' will do wonders for morale and standards.

Most important, the very parents whom teachers need to see about their children seldom attend meetings or open days. High priority to attendance at such meetings is a common feature of successful schools.

Little of this disadvantage will be solved by nutrition alone. In any case, levels of nutrition generally are not much different between social classes. The quality of food and its freshness, and the range of fruit and vegetables eaten, are probably where differences lie. Poor-quality food is one small part of a cloud that hangs over the disadvantaged to baulk the development of potential intelligence and self-esteem. Only the widest policy involving education, employment and health will improve a worsening situation.

References

1 W. A. Marshall, 'Growth in children: the tall child', *Update* **3** (1972).

2 Richard Lynn, 'A nutrition theory of the secular increases in intelligence . . .', *British Journal of Educational Psychology* **59** (1989).

3 Joseph Kay, *The Social Conditions and Education of the People in England and Europe* (London, 1850).

4 Department of Health, *On the State of the Public Health for the Year 1988* (HMSO, 1989).

Chapter 10

GROWTH AND HEALTH

Over a century ago it was observed by a wise doctor that to do things to a child that promote a good growth rate also blesses a child with the ability to resist infection. His general perceptiveness about the link between growth and health has been confirmed many times and recently detail has been added as to causes. It must be stressed once more that there is a world of difference between a person who is small and who reaches his genetic potential for height and another who is small because of poverty or disease. It is the latter that is our concern – smallness as a symptom of something wrong rather than smallness as a 'possession' as J. M. Tanner puts it.

Of course, much investigation of the relationship between growth and health comes from the study of *groups* of people. Comparisons of groups brings out average differences and their magnitude. As a result specific questions can be asked about such differences, and at the wish of society programmes can be devised that concentrate and compensate for group handicap. However, in attacking social problems the quite necessary concentration on average differences should never divert attention from the *individual*, who is the proper unit of our concern.

Through comparisons of groups it is known that shorter people, on average, have a higher mortality at all ages until the over-70s. This is not good news for those children who are stunted by disease and poverty in their early life. This is not as serious a problem here as in developing countries, but it exists and is a cause for shame.

Trends to lower heights are found where the father has a manual occupation or where the father is unemployed, or where children have free school meals or the family receives supplementary benefit (see Table 2.1, p. 19). It is in these groups that health problems multiply.

The evidence for these bleak statements comes partly from Norway and England. In the mid-1960s all people in Norway over 15 were X-rayed as part of a screening programme and their heights and weights were recorded. All told, 1.8 million people were examined and by 1984 176,000 of these had died. In each age group below the over-70s the highest mortality rate occurred among the shorter people. A possible clue to the cause of this is that the most of the 1960 adult population in Norway were born in the 1920s and 1930s when poverty was more common.

The other piece of evidence comes from two Whitehall studies[1] of civil servants (in 1969 and 1988) which showed a three-fold difference in mortality between the lowest and highest grades. The latter are the tallest, the former the shortest, and it is these who have the higher death rates (see Table 10.1).

These differences in height reflect differences in social class. The tallest on *average* are the civil service mandarins, the shortest the clerical and other grades – social grades one and six, respectively. The higher grades are much healthier than their clerical colleagues in the lowest grades, a pattern reflected in the social classes of society in general. The finger of suspicion is pointed once again at the possible effects of early life environment – poverty. There are also clear employment-grade differences in life-style which affect health: smoking, diet and exercise; differences in economic circumstance, in social circumstances at work (monotony and low job satisfaction), and in social support.

Poverty in early life

What do these shorter people actually suffer from or die of, and what are the critical times when environmental circumstances impinge to affect long-term health? What specific features of the environment are harmful? Some pointers to the answers of these complex questions have been made by Professor D. J. P. Barker's team at Southampton University, and by others. In brief, the answers to the three questions are: coronary heart disease, stroke, diabetes, asthma and chronic bronchitis; pregnancy and the first year of life; poverty at the time of birth and infancy.

Table 10.1 Relative mortality by civil service grade and cause of death

Cause of death	Admin.	Relative mortality Professional/ executive	Clerical	Other
Lung cancer	0.5	1.0	2.2	3.6
Other cancer	0.8	1.0	1.4	1.4
CHD	0.6	1.0	1.4	1.7
Cerebrovascular disease	0.3	1.0	1.4	1.2
Other cardiovascular	0.9	1.0	1.4	2.0
Chronic bronchitis	0	1.0	6.0	7.3
Other respiratory	1.1	1.0	2.6	3.1
Gastrointestinal disease	0	1.0	1.6	2.8
Genitourinary disease	1.3	1.0	0.7	3.1
Accident and violence	0	1.0	1.4	1.5
Suicide	0.7	1.0	1.0	1.9
Other deaths	0	1.0	1.9	2.0
Causes not related to smoking				
Cancer	0.8	1.0	1.3	1.4
Non-cancer	0.6	1.0	1.5	2.0
All causes	0.6	1.0	1.6	2.1

Source: Adapted from a table in 'Inequalities in death – specific explanations of a general pattern?' by M. G. Marmot *et al.* (*Lancet*, 5 May 1984).

Barker *et al.*[2] struck on the idea of using records of date of birth, birth weight, weight at one year, and also whether babies were bottle- or breast-fed, and relating these to cause of death. Nearly 6,000 men born in Hertfordshire between 1911 and 1930 were traced, and the outcome was clear. Men with the lowest birth weight (2.5 kg or less) *and* lowest weight at one year (9 kg or less) had the highest death rates from ischaemic heart disease (IHD) (poor blood flow through the coronary arteries leading to angina and heart attack). By contrast the lowest death rates occurred in men who had above-average birth weight *or* weight at one year. Over 90 per cent of the babies were breast-fed so these findings cannot be applied to bottle-fed babies.

As Chapters 4 and 5 explained, growth, both during pregnancy and afterwards, determines the weight at a year, and processes linked to growth, and acting at these times, appear to strongly influence the risk of heart disese. Promotion of good growth in babies of below-average birth weight will be beneficial to long-term health. Heavier weight at age 1 is also accompanied by large reductions in death rates. Among babies with above-average birth weight the risk of heart disease is below average, irrespective of infant growth, but the *combined* risks of LBW *and* low weight at age 1 are serious.

It looks as if some adult illness at least is the result of poor conditions in pregnancy and in early life and takes 50 or 60 years to manifest itself. Birth weight is also strongly affected by the mother's height, which itself is largely determined by growth in early childhood and this in turn by quality of environment. Poverty has much to answer for and its time-bomb effect is worrying.

But how does poverty affect development in the uterus to trigger poor health in later life? Barker thinks that poor maternal nutrition could restrict the development of vital organs in the foetus. The foetus is not like a clock that ticks at a fixed rate. It makes 'trade-offs'. If nutrition is restricted, the foetus will divert what is available to those organs of the most immediate importance and away from organs that will not become important until later in life. Specifically, brain growth is given priority over trunk growth. Such trade-offs imposed by an adverse environment will have long-term effects on physiology and metabolism and may lead to mid-life illnesses such as heart disease and diabetes.

Birth weight and other adult illness

The guilt of poverty as one major cause of later ills is strengthened by other evidence. Stroke[3] is linked (in a statistical sense) with LBW and a negative relationship exists between birth weight and blood pressure: the lower the birth weight, *on average*, the higher the pressure in adult life.

This relationship suggests that poor conditions in the uterus during pregnancy lead to poor growth of the foetus. The link between this and high blood pressure is obscure but pressure could be increased by the higher force necessary to maintain blood flow across the placenta (which may enlarge with poor nutrition, as mentioned in Chapter 3), and the raised pressure could persist after birth.

Thankfully deaths from stroke have fallen over the past 40 years, which is consistent with past improvements in maternal health and physique and greater reproductive efficiency.

The seeds of chronic bronchitis[4] are often sown in poverty in perhaps the first year of life due to lung infection then. Overcrowding, poor housing, poor nutrition, poor infant feeding practices and smoking are the soil from which this illness springs. Conditions have, of course, vastly improved but there is still cause for concern for a proportion, perhaps 10 per cent of children, reared in poor conditions in the UK.

A puzzle remains to be explained. The incidence of stroke has fallen but why has coronary heart disease (CHD) risen so steeply in recent years when it should be generally falling in rate with higher standards of living?

The future health of schoolchildren

CHD may have two causes: one acting through the mother or in infancy which is linked to poverty, the other acting in adult life which is associated with affluence.[5] We must wait and see what happens to the present generation of schoolchildren in the early twenty-first century when they are 30 and 40. The life-styles of some children, largely of the lower social classes, do not augur well: sloth, a high-fat diet, a deficiency of fresh fruit and vegetables, with smoking as a habit in up to 20 per cent of teenagers. Add to these factors poor circumstances in early life leading to low birth weight in, say, 10 per cent and the picture darkens. Already information suggests that the prevalence of unhealthy life-styles among the poor (smoking, less well-balanced diet and obesity) contributes to the differential in life expectancy between social classes.

References

1 M. G. Marmot, M. J. Shipley and G. Rose, 'Inequalities in death', *Lancet* (5 May 1984).

2 D. J. P. Barker, C. Osmond, P. Winter, B. Margetts and J. Simmonds, 'Weight in infancy and death from ischaemic heart disease', *Lancet* (9 September 1989).

3 D. J. P. Barker and C. Osmond, 'Death rates from stroke', *British Medical Journal* **295** (1987).

4 D. J. P. Barker and C. Osmond, 'Childhood respiratory infection. . .', *British Medical Journal* **293** (1986).

5 D. J. P. Barker, 'Childhood causes of adult diseases', *Archives of Diseases in Childhood* **63** (1988).

Chapter 11

SOME HEALTH IMPLICATIONS FOR SCHOOLCHILDREN

Much of what I have said in Chapters 7 and 8 about diet calls for comment but there are a few other issues mentioned in passing that I want to develop.

Fat

I have referred to the fact that too much fat is eaten by children: 75 per cent of all children consumed more than 35 per cent of their energy as fat and some children took more than 50 per cent.[1] There has been much public debate about the dietary risk factors in coronary heart disease (CHD), notably saturated (hard) and polyunsaturated (soft) fats, cholesterol, and to a lesser extent sugar. Besides these risk factors, heredity, cigarette smoking, sloth, diabetes, high blood pressure and overweight must play a part. But in the medley of risks there is a danger that one (e.g. fat) will be taken up with enthusiasm and pushed without taking into account other unknown or suspected risks. Suffice it to say that the causes of CHD are multiple and only half-understood.

Nevertheless, it is well-established that arterial disease can start in early childhood. Fatty streaks have been found in the coronary arteries of babies of a few months old and they become common at 5. They may be reabsorbed and vanish at this age but the raised patches which arise on the artery walls of some people later in life may have their origins in these fatty streaks. The raised patches can lead to the arteries becoming blocked by one or more processes: slow furring up, blood clots, or splitting of the arterial wall.

With regard to fat it is the saturated fats which seem to be the major culprit in heart disease because they tend to raise blood cholesterol levels; and the obstructive narrowing of the arteries just mentioned is associated with deposition of cholesterol on the artery walls and CHD. It is well known that the higher the blood cholesterol level in an individual the greater the risk of heart disease.

Saturated fats are contained in meat, lard, suet, eggs and dairy products. The polyunsaturated fats are contained in corn oil, peanuts and soya beans and are among the chief sources of fat for the manufacture of margarine. Fatty fish such as herring, sardine and mackerel are also rich in polyunsaturates. These fats do not seem to be linked to heart disease and may even have a protective effect by lowering cholesterol levels.

The average proportion of polyunsaturated to saturated fats (the P/S ratio) in the whole diet is now about 0.37, having risen from about 0.22 in 1977 and 0.20 in 1970. This rise in the ratio of polyunsaturated to saturated fats eaten is mainly due to a switch from red to white meat, from whole to skimmed milk, and from butter to margarine. The official Committee on the Medical Aspects of Food Policy (COMA) set a relatively low target of 0.45 for the P/S ratio but there is obviously a long way to go to meet it. How far is shown by the fact that the recent Department of Health report on diet[2] recommends that saturated fats should provide an average for the population of only 10 per cent of total dietary energy. At present, saturated fats make up about 16 per cent of this energy – an average figure that must conceal some very high percentages. Only 5 per cent of the UK population derives 10 per cent of energy or less from saturated fat. To shift the vast bulk of the population to the official recommendation would need a sea change in eating habits and in policies for food manufacture and animal breeding. Nevertheless, reducing levels of blood cholesterol would, it is suggested, make 'substantial' reductions in the risks of CHD.

For our purposes, children in particular need to cut down on saturated fats. At present, three-quarters of children have intakes of total fats over the official recommendation of 35 per cent of their energy intake. Milk and chips are the two main contributors to fat intakes. The poor are particularly affected.

Though changes in diet can reduce concentrations of blood cholesterol, and in turn CHD, food is not is chief source. Only about 15 per cent of all blood cholesterol comes from the diet.

The liver is the main producer. Any deficiency in blood cholesterol is compensated for by the liver making more of its own. High levels of saturated fat in the diet, however, seem to encourage the liver to produce larger amounts of cholesterol. This process can be reversed if the total level of saturated fat in the diet is reduced. So the best way to reduce the amount of blood cholesterol is to lower intake of all kinds of fats, particularly saturated fats. Excess cholesterol is got rid of through the excretory system of the liver and gall bladder.

High blood cholesterol levels, then, seem to be *chiefly* due to a person's inherited make-up: in the way an individual's body handles fat, rather than the nature of their diet. For example, the reduction of saturated fat from 16 per cent to 10 per cent of dietary energy (a large reduction) would result in a decrease of blood cholesterol concentration of only about 0.4 mmol/1.[2] The official aim is for it to be less than 5.2 mmol/1. Two-thirds of the British population are above this, and the average concentration in the UK is something in the order of 5.8 mmol/1.

There is no conclusive evidence at present that dietary fat plays a part in cancer deaths but the evidence that is available cautions against high-fat diets. Nevertheless, the vitamin/cancer link has become stronger. Sir Richard Doll,[3] a world authority on cancer, has said:

> there is much more evidence [than about fat] about the value of fruit and green vegetables in the prevention of various types of cancer, including stomach cancer and large bowel cancer. There is quite good evidence that beta-carotene is protective, although the effect is not dramatic. If one has to pick out a particular nutrient then it is beta-carotene that stands out, although vitamin C may well be helpful in preventing stomach cancer.

Beta-carotene is contained in yellow fruits and vegetables: carrots, swedes, tomatoes, apricots, with mustard and cress and watercress containing plenty, though the orange colour is masked by the green pigment chlorophyll. Vitamin C is contained in citrus fruits and potatoes.

Heredity plays a big part in heart disease and probably in cancer. Nothing can be done about a person's heredity except, as George Bernard Shaw said, to choose our parents wisely. By getting the life-style right the balance can be tipped in our favour. It is important to:

1 *Feed children sensibly.* School meals provide, on average, 40 per cent of energy from fat while the *weekly* diet attracts about the same, though some children have diets where 50 per cent of energy is derived from fat. Provided that the energy intakes are maintained *there is scope for the improvement of diet by reducing the total fat content of school meals, and those eaten at home and in snacks, to give about 35 per cent of the total energy contributed by fat. Nutritional standards for school meals should be reintroduced.*

2 *Teach children sensible eating habits from an early age*: the value of a good mixed diet to include cereal foods, protein foods, some fat, fruit and vegetables (including pulses). Biscuits, cakes, sweets, fizzy drinks, burgers, chips and crisps should not displace more useful food too often.

3 *Give some understanding to children of social, political and economic issues such as the fluoridation of water and the labelling of foods.*

4 *Encourage regular exercise at school and home*, especially that which gives pleasure after school and beyond. The dietary survey[1] shows that children's calorie intakes are about 10 per cent lower than DHSS recommendations and reflect a decrease in physical activity rather than undernutrition. Lack of activity is not expected as a feature of the life of young children, who naturally explore and play tirelessly unless they are ill. At nursery school, however, a 4- or 5-year-old can spend much time sitting – as do primary and secondary children. Many children spend about 24 hours a week watching TV. Mostly, because of road conditions, they rightly do not walk to school. Whether the intensity of physical education at school (now a compulsory subject) raises the heart rate sufficiently to protect the heart is to be doubted.[4] In any case, primary schools have, in general, poor resources for physical education and in secondary schools there is less time for sport and extra-curricular activities involving physical education. In part this is due to pressures

on time from the National Curriculum, where physical education is often last in the queue.

The critical factor in cardiovascular training in children involves raising the heart rate to about 140 beats per minute, which is approximately between 60 per cent and 85 per cent of the maximum rate, and then maintaining it for ten minutes. This is equivalent to a brisk walk at between five and six miles per hour. Achieving this level through activity three times per week for twenty minutes is the ideal and needs to be one of the aims of school PE.

One study of adolescents showed that half the children tested did not sustain the 150 beats per minute for any ten-minute period over the period of testing. Another study showed that 83 per cent of a sample of 500 adolescents were involved in less than five minutes of vigorous activity per day.[4] 'Vigorous' was defined as becoming sweaty or breathless during the exercise.

A combination of sensible eating and physical activity is protective against heart disease, obesity and osteoporosis. To protect the heart the exercise has to be regular and aerobic, using the big muscles of the body more vigorously than is customary. PE and games, brisk walking, cycling and swimming are protective. Any form of activity is helpful in preventing obesity. For bone strength the activity has to be weight-bearing such as walking. In general, a healthier diet is gaining ground but exercise is declining. This is a cause for concern as probably half the risk of heart attack is due to lack of exercise.

Obesity

Obesity (20 per cent overweight for height and build) is not common in primary school children though about 6 per cent are fat and it is at adolescence that the percentage rises, especially among girls. Its causes are complex but the degree of obesity in parents and grandparents, plus its severity in puberty, are the most important pointers to weight level in adult life. The roots of much illness and early death appear to lie in childhood obesity. Of about 500 children aged 0–16 admitted to hospital (in Sweden) for obesity, higher proportions suffered illness in adult life and died young compared with the proportions in the general population.[5] For example, about 16 per cent of 10–20-year-olds had heart problems, compared with about 0.3 per cent in the general population. At aged 30 to 40 years, 26 per cent had heart disease compared with about 3 per cent generally. The mean age of death was 41 (one of the most accurate predictors of a man's life expectancy is his waist measurement at 40: the fewer the inches the longer the life). *Weight-reducing measures started early in life under good medical care are vital.* Schools can, if necessary, draw parents' attention to the need for such care early on.

Dental caries

This remains one of the most common childhood diseases, causing pain and discomfort and affecting well-being and appearance. In 1983, by the age of 5, about half of the children in the UK had one or more decayed teeth, this rising to 93 per cent of 15-year-olds. *Poor oral hygiene and sugars are the most important factors in the cause of dental caries,*[6] but not those sugars naturally incorporated in fresh fruits, vegetables and starchy foods. Soft drinks, sweets, biscuits, cakes and puddings are obviously harmful in excess and should be replaced by those foods just mentioned. The official panel's report recommended that schools should 'promote nutritionally sound food choices'.[6] Most schools know this, but progress is slow. Like others in this list it is one of the many examples of social/health problems that are laid by society on the doorstep of schools.

Smoking

Maternal smoking during pregnancy has been shown (Chapter 4) to correlate with lower birth weight with its associated risks, and thereafter with shorter height in childhood and increased prevalence of respiratory complaints. There is also a relationship between passive smoking and a reduction in birth weight.

Currently, about 32 per cent of the population smoke cigarettes – 33 per cent of men and 30 per cent of women. This proportion, though high, has fallen from 45 per cent in 1974.[7] Most smokers take up regular smoking before the age of 18.

About 8 per cent of children aged 11 to 15 in England and about 17 per cent of 15- and 16-year-old boys and 22 per cent of girls smoke regularly. Smoking is responsible for 90 per cent of lung cancer deaths, 20 per cent of heart disease deaths, and 90 per cent of deaths from bronchitis and related illness – perhaps 100,000 deaths a year. Looked at in a more general way, in developed countries like Britain tobacco causes about 30 per cent of *all* premature deaths (between the ages of 35 and 69).[8]

Smoking is the largest preventable cause of disease and premature death in the UK. Giving up smoking is the single most important step a person can take to improve his/her health.

Drugs

Alcohol and cigarettes are two of the commonest social drugs used by schoolchildren. Most heads regard alcohol use as a much more serious problem than the use of illicit drugs and medicines. Drinking by schoolchildren starts at about 12 or 13. Lunch-time drinking by older boys is a problem in some schools. Drinking by the young reflects increased drinking by adults, and between 1970 and 1988 alcohol consumption per head rose by nearly 40 per cent.[7] *If alcohol is consumed to excess or at the wrong time it can cause significant physical, psychological and social harm.* A high proportion of teenage injuries and road accidents are attributable to the misuse of alcohol. For example, 25 per cent of teenage drivers killed in road traffic accidents in 1985 had blood samples exceeding the limit for alcohol; and hospital casualty departments often see teenage boys with injuries due to drunken brawls.

With regard to timing, if a pregnant mother smokes, takes aspirin, tranquillisers or any other drug, and regularly enjoys alcohol, the risks to her baby increase and the long-term effects may hamper a child's school work. The foetus is most sensitive to drugs in the first three months of life (Chapter 3). *Drugs or medicines should be taken during pregnancy only when necessary, and that will be rare.*

German measles (rubella)

Infection of a pregnant mother by German measles is a well-known hazard to the embryo (Chapter 1), and children can be born with eye and other defects. *All schoolgirls should be vaccinated by their fourteenth birthday* (about 90 per cent now are).[9]

Lead poisoning

Lead in petrol has become linked with the impairment of children's behaviour and intelligence. The evidence for this is increasing but it is unlikely that lead at low concentrations could be more than a minor factor itself in pulling down IQ. Nevertheless, *in combination with poor family life and bad food and housing, low lead levels add their effect to impair the brain*. The removal of lead from petrol will add to the safety margin for some children who live in areas polluted by lead in plumbing, paint, and industrial waste. Action to remove lead from petrol, paint and plumbing was recommended by a Royal Commission Report.[10] Because petrol was the most clearly identifiable source the Report recommended that unleaded petrol should be available by 1990. Unleaded petrol is now a choice, and is significantly cheaper than leaded petrol. The government was also asked to encourage the replacement of lead plumbing and to reduce the permissible quantities of lead in paint.

References

1 DHSS, *The Diets of British School Children* (HMSO, 1989).
2 Department of Health, *Dietary Reference Values for Food, etc.* (HMSO, 1991).
3 Richard Doll, quoted in *The Times* (5 October 1989).
4 DES, *Education and Health* (HMSO, 1986).
5 Hans-Olaf Mossberg, '40-year follow up of overweight children', *Lancet* (26 September 1989).
6 Department of Health, *Dietary Sugars and Human Disease* (HMSO, 1989).
7 Department of Health, *The Health of the Nation* (HMSO, 1991).
8 Richard Peto *et al.*, 'Mortality from tobacco in developed countries', *Lancet* (23 May 1992).
9 Department of Health, *On the State of the Public Health for the Year 1988* (HMSO, 1989).
10 DHSS, *Lead in the Environment* (HMSO, 1983).

Chapter 12

ADVERSITY

It is useful to draw together some of the factors referred to earlier which may adversely affect growth and the related aspects of intelligence, emotional development and physical health in later life. These 'adverse' effects, acting singly or in combination at a critical time, will diminish the realisation of a child's potential and if they continue they produce a disaster.

Disadvantage, in an educational sense, is provided by a home devoid of love and stimulus that affects a child's mental, physical and emotional development. Disadvantage in this sense has, of course, little to do with economics. A 'poor' home in the economic sense may have plenty of affection, talk and things to do, and may also provide a child with the ability to solve problems. Indeed, much evidence and common experience show that the father's income and job, poor housing and drab surroundings are of less importance for success at school than the interest shown by parents in a child's work and progress. The Court Report[1] had this to say about disadvantaged children:

Children who grow up in poverty or squalor, whose homes are grossly overcrowded, or who live in decaying inner-city neighbourhoods; children who are neglected or handicapped, or who are discriminated against on grounds of race, language, colour or religion; children whose parents are sick or psychiatrically disordered, who quarrel incessantly – or who are absent; such children are in different ways 'disadvantaged'. The term has no precise meaning, but the implication is clear enough. Social or personal disadvantage is handicapping and dysfunctional. Of course many children who are disadvantaged personally or socially may develop normally and function adequately. But they face greater odds than other children: they are more likely to suffer from physical illness or psychiatric disorder, or to fail educationally, or to drop out of school or be 'early leavers', more likely to truant or become delinquent, or to leave school for unemployment or poorly skilled jobs.

Though fifteen years old the report is still relevant in the 1990s. Indeed the situation has worsened. The gap between rich and poor and North and South is widening. Schooling in the state system deteriorates while independent schools flourish.

Indices of disadvantage

Classically, the kind of disadvantage described exists in its concentrate form in the city slum. In lesser concentration it exists on bleak housing estates in town and country, in rural cottages, on isolated farms, and even in executive homes in commuter-belt country.

In a physical sense the infant mortality rate and the height of children at a given age can be used as a measure of disadvantage, provided it is understood that both measures are considered in relation to averages of groups of children rather than for individuals, in whom allowances have to be made for hereditary differences. Broadly speaking, differences in nourishment and care influence both. Overcrowding, dirt, poor food and bad housing, a father out of work, ignorant parents and broken homes, all send up the average mortality rate. For many of the same reasons, the average heights of children of manual and non-manual workers show a 2-cm gap at age 3 and a 5-cm gap at adolescence. While most urban communities contain a mass of disadvantaged children, infant mortality and height indices are related more closely to social class and availability of facilities than to 'town' or 'country'.

None of this physical evidence tells us much about the effects of neglect on the intellect or emotions, and knowledge on this subject is sparse. There are, however, certain environmental influences which are likely to hamper growth and development and with this the intellect and perhaps the emotions. Although these are given separately, each is difficult to isolate as a cause of low intellect and poor character, for most belong to a syndrome of poverty and, of course, to heredity.

Malnutrition

It is important to distinguish between the chronic malnutrition common in the Third World and malnutrition acting as part of poor conditions of life in relatively affluent countries like the UK and USA. In the first instance, children are commonly born with low birth weights, grow poorly through most or all of their childhood, with many not achieving their genetic potential for height thus remaining stunted. With the double disadvantage of malnutrition in pregnancy and early childhood, there is little doubt that such undernourished children are poor achievers in later life.

In the second instance malnutrition belongs to a complex picture of disadvantage in which poor food now plays a small part – in having a LBW for example. This may not have been the case 50 or more years ago when poverty was more widespread, with the associated, long-term consequences to health and intellect.

There is little evidence that children in the UK are now shorter through malnutrition alone. Class differences in height, which start to operate at age 2 and persist, appear to have multiple causes but certainly the diet of the poor is worse in *quality* than that of the rich.

The dietary survey[2] shows, for example, that children's nutrient intakes are not much affected by their being in families receiving benefits, by social class, or by being in a one- or two-parent family – though daily energy intakes for children are much higher in social classes I and II than in IV and V. The mean vitamin C intake of 10-year-old boys from class I is over 12 mg/day higher than that of boys from social class V. Among the former, 27 per cent of vitamin C comes from fruit juice, 17 per cent from vegetables and less than 15 per cent from chips; in contrast, class V boys derive 21 per cent from chips and less than 15 per cent from both fruit and vegetables.

The mean calcium intake of boys from class I is higher by 120 mg/day than that of boys from class V. Milk is the major contributor of calcium and such vitamins as vitamin B6 (pyridoxine). Differences in milk drunk is reflected in the fall with social class of mean intakes of these nutrients.

With 10-year-old girls there is a similar story. Girls from

social class V (or with unemployed fathers) obtained over twice as much of their fat, vitamin C, iron and thiamin from chips than those for class I, while getting only about 75 per cent as much fat, calcium and vitamin B6 from their milk. In fact 11 per cent of total energy is obtained from chips by 10-year-old girls in class V and with unemployed fathers compared with 5 per cent from class I. By contrast, 9 per cent of total energy is contributed by milk to girls from class I but only 6 per cent for girls from class V and from homes with an unemployed father.

Nevertheless, the facts show that children of all classes, plus those with fathers who are unemployed and those of one-parent families, do not differ greatly in their nutrient intake. Protein, vitamin and mineral intake is close to the Recommended Daily Amount (RDA), although large numbers of children of all classes and social circumstances are below the RDA for iron.

It seems that it is in the quality of food, its freshness, and the range of fruit and vegetables eaten where differences lie between richer and poorer. Heart disease, obesity and bowel cancer (associated with eating too much saturated fat, sugar and salt and too little fibre) appear to be diseases of poverty. It is the poor who also smoke too much.

A plate of Brussel sprouts, liver and boiled potatoes, followed by stewed apple, is nourishing but not particularly attractive to children compared with sausage, baked beans and chips followed by ice cream. George Orwell knew about the importance to the poor of 'tasty' food. He wrote in *The Road to Wigan Pier*:

> The ordinary human being would rather starve than live on brown bread and raw carrots, and the peculiar evil is this, that the less money you have, the less inclined you feel to spend it on wholesome food. A millionaire may enjoy breakfasting off orange juice and Ryvita biscuits ... [but] When you are underfed, harassed, bored and miserable, you want something a little bit 'tasty'.

With young children under 5, when, as emphasised in this book, they are learning at an enormous pace, the National Children's Home (NCH)[3] has produced evidence that families using NCH centres are struggling to bring up their children on very low incomes. A picture is painted of parents regularly going hungry themselves in order to feed their children and of large numbers of children eating nutritionally poor diets. Fatty meat and meat products are eaten more often than lean meat and fish. Less than half the children and almost two-thirds of the parents did not eat fruit or green vegetables every day while three-quarters of the families never ate brown or wholemeal bread. Nevertheless, half the children ate sweets and savoury snacks every day. Crisps and sweets are very cheap sources of calories compared with fruit and vegetables. For example, two custard cream biscuits or a bag of crisps give a hundred calories and cost 3p and 12p respectively. Three small apples give a hundred calories but cost 29p (1989 prices).

From all that has been said earlier it is clear that the quality of what children eat is vital in determining how well they will be during their lives and indeed, as Chapter 10 showed, may play a part in how long they live. The constraints of poverty, however, make quality hard to achieve. Price, limited cooking and storage facilities in bed and breakfast accommodation, and lack of long-term interest in health – all restrict what can be given to children. As a general rule 'the less the money, the lower the morale and the shorter perspective on health'.[4] In April 1992 the Institute for Fiscal Studies reported that since 1979 tax and benefit changes had given an average of £87 a week to the richest 10 per cent while the poorest 10 per cent lost £1 a week. A 1990 government survey[5] stated that from 1981 to 1987 average incomes rose ten times as fast as the incomes of the poorest 10 per cent. Behind these figures lie children who are generally badly educated and fed and living in stressful conditions.

Smoking

This has been commented on in Chapters 4 and 11, and the attendant risks described. The social classes differ in their smoking habits, the lower social classes smoking more. Its effects will be additive to those of poor-quality food.

Lack of sleep

Sleep may be important to give the brain 'the rest it deserves' after the immense barrage of information fed into it in the day, but the amount of sleep needed is variable and a child is only not getting enough if he or she is tired the next day. Some physiologists claim that those nerve cells which are the seat of intensive activity during the day, and where chemical change goes on, need to recover. In short, sleep may be a period of maintenance and repair of the nerve cell networks used in memory and learning. In the young, where new synapses are being formed and the wiring of the brain is changing, sleep is of very great importance. Though there is a lack of hard information we all know from experience that 'sleeping on it' helps to clarify and consolidate thoughts.

Noise

The type which can reduce sleep and concentration may affect the brain though this is uncertain; children can enjoy noise and commotion and 'switch off' when need be.

Anxiety

This may affect memory and concentration. In school there can be an anxiety to please, to give the 'right' answer in class, while worries about home conditions can lead to school refusal. If, for example, there has been a row, and the mother threatens to run away or to commit suicide, then the child will be afraid to leave his mother in case something happens to her. Most truancy is not due to this, but some will be.

Pollution of the environment by lead

This has been dealt with in Chapter 11.

Lack of opportunities for exploration and play in young children

Lack of such opportunities and associated language development may damage the mind as much as smoking damages the heart and lungs. 'Shut-up' answers to questions, lack of dialogue and of opportunities for broader conversation, such as family meals, may hamper development as may harsh work regimes on isolated farms where children may be alone for long periods. In some rural areas, isolation from conversation and from other children may be significant factors in hampering human achievement, though generalisation is dangerous. A mother in a city may be as isolated in a tower block, and if the lift breaks down her small child may be as deprived of opportunities for play and language as a child living in rural isolation.

A poor start in family life

A poor start affects general development, intellect, and emotional and social progress. Although most children are healthy and have caring homes, many live in divided or broken homes. Many families live in physically unsatisfactory conditions: overcrowding, poor housing, bed and breakfast accommodation and sharing. Bad housing can exacerbate an already tense family situation.

The Court Report[1] sums all this up: 'There is now extensive evidence that an adverse family and social environment can retard physical, emotional and intellectual growth, lead to more frequent and more serious illness and aversely affect educational achievement and personal behaviour.'

It is hardly surprising that many studies of slow learners in secondary schools in the last twenty years found that adverse social conditions were widespread among these educationally retarded pupils.

Why is family life important to the child? The quality of language, play and schooling a child experiences depends very much on the vitality and interactiveness of a family: chat, outings, games, help with school work – and interest in it – and so on; security, self-reliance and self-esteem flow from it as well.

A great diversity of family patterns exists: nuclear, extended, one-parent, children living with grandparents and so on. For all of these patterns the family has (or should have) a protective function. Ideally it serves as a secure base from which a child can explore and test out his environment.

The family environment provides immediate and early models of behaviour for a child to observe and imitate, and, later on, school provides them too. Observational learning must have been of special importance in the development of the human brain and behaviour. Because we are born with a relatively poor non-learning behaviour repertoire such learning is a crucial part of family life. A child's way of coping with, for example, stress, by either passive resignation or anger, will be influenced by the way his parents cope. Inter-personal relationships, how decisions are made, and attitudes to work seem likely to be influenced similarly by 'role modelling'. Parents' relationships will to a large extent serve as a model for their children's own relationships with the opposite sex.

Observation of verbal and physical aggression is likely to lead to similar behaviour in children witnessing it. Nursery school children allowed to see adults exhibiting such aggression to a doll are subsequently likely to behave with similar aggression towards it, whereas children who have seen adults behaving neutrally towards the doll are not. This particular example of observational learning has relevance to controversial subjects such as the role of television on violence. Unfortunately, extraordinarily little is known about the permanence or reversibility of such early learning.

Ideally, the family helps to release a child's potential. A child has no way himself of releasing this potential, but the interaction between the child and the family helps him to grow and develop well.

With regard to the release of potential and developing self-esteem a child credits his parents (the blood-tie is not important) with extraordinary wisdom. If they behave as if he is valuable he takes these actions as evidence of his essential goodness. On the other hand, if they behave as if he is without worth he begins to wonder about his capacity to be valued by someone else.

A good family life allows the first personal relationships between mother, father, and brothers and sisters and the baby to develop. The close 'bonding' between an infant and its mother needs to be successfully established; indeed, it is being increasingly appreciated that this bonding is important in determining the way the child relates to others inside the family and later to those outside the family circle. Many of the factors which allow secure attachments between mother and child are, however, obscure and disruptions of attachment may occur for many reasons, including genetic or other defects in the child itself. It is not always the parent's fault.

The family also sets standards of morality, so that a child knows what is right or wrong and what is acceptable or refused. He can then establish his own standards. It is also a refuge, a known territory private from the world outside, a place where it is known how far to go and who is sensitive about what. It can give moral and material support in times of adversity.

I have idealised the role of the family. It is true that family life has its negative, oppressive and even brutal elements, but the positive qualities mentioned outweigh them and have helped Man to survive as a species. Indeed, perhaps the large frontal areas of the brain are very much concerned with the qualities of unselfishness, of restraint, and with the need to co-operate, and are there for us to learn to use.

While the nuclear family is the most common pattern, one must remember lone-parent families of which there are large numbers. Numbers are difficult to estimate, but in Great Britain in 1987 the proportion of one-parent families, for whatever reason, was one in seven. For some inner-city areas it may be nearer one in three. Most are headed by a divorced or separated wife.

The effect of a single-parent family on a child's upbringing is not always poor. Single parents, whether mother or father, are often marvellous at bringing up children by themselves. There is even some evidence that when a mother remarries the health and education of the child deteriorate because more attention goes to the stepfather and not enough to the child.

With regard to child battering, environmental conditions such as bad housing can worsen a tense family situation, and families of children battered by their parents often live in poor housing: houses where doors open straight onto busy roads, where there is little or no garden for children to play in, where a crying child disturbs neighbours so that the mother always has to be on the watch, where a mother spends her day in a tower-block flat because the lift has stuck or she is afraid of being attacked.

Coping and stress

Coping with day-to-day family affairs is part and parcel of family living. It can give spice to life, or it can lead to illness and exhaustion.

There are other stresses in family life, not all unpleasant: a parent working hard to acquire more of the trappings of affluence such as a new car; a marriage; a child passing an examination, and so on.

Each one of us has a stress limit beyond which our coping powers fail. It is not clear how the brain brings about the adaptations associated with coping. One is the redistribution of blood flow to the 'thinking' areas of the brain; there is also increased nervous activity. Nervous arousal helps the brain to think more quickly. The trouble is that high arousal can lead to poor sleep, whereas success in working out a solution to the problem brings satisfaction, lowers the level of nervous arousal and allows sleep. Poor nights, if repeated in succession due to high arousal of the nervous system, can lead to exhaustion of the coping system. Stress in family life can have this effect with spin-off on a child's work at school and on his general attitude.

References

1 DHSS, *Fit for the Future* (HMSO, 1976).
2 DHSS, *The Diets of British School Children* (HMSO, 1989).
3 National Children's Homes, *Poverty and Nutrition Survey* (NCH, 1991).
4 Health Education Authority, *Diet, Nutrition and Healthy Eating in Low Income Groups* (HEA, 1989).
5 Department of Social Security, *Households below Average Income* (HMSO, 1990).

Chapter 13

SCHOOL

The last chapter stressed the importance of the family in exploiting (or not) the critical periods of development. School is another major influence, although without the understanding, co-operation and participation of parents, school time is not as productive as it might be. The time a child between the ages of 5 and 16 spends at school is about 17 per cent of his waking hours. Children who go to a half-day nursery school from their third to fifth birthday spend about 4 per cent of their waking time of the first five years of life at school. Not much. Co-operation between parents and school will magnify school effects and children will have a better chance by good co-operation. The use of the multiple critical times which happen during the starting school years will be enhanced by parent–school links.

The goals of education for all children are the same and those given by the Warnock Report[1] are worth restating. These are: to enlarge a child's knowledge, experience and imaginative understanding and thus his awareness of moral values and capacity for enjoyment; and to enable him to enter the world, after formal education is completed, in order to take his part in society, to be a responsible contributor to it and to be able to stand on his own feet. For a few, the road towards these twin goals is easy, but for most it is rough though possible; for some it is strewn with the obstacles of handicap of body and mind.

To fill out these generalities a few details are important. They are covered in the following paragraphs.

Quality of head and staff

The head is the single most important influence in the success or failure of a school. It was ever thus. Matthew Arnold knew from his own inspections over a century ago that the 'character of the Master' was a crucial factor for good or ill. Imagination and vision tempered by realism are key attributes for assessing what should be done *now* and for knowing what is likely to be attained in the future. The head's character *creates* that all-important climate of feeling in a school, whether of enterprise and co-operation or of pin-pricking and uncertainty, and this sets standards of work and behaviour.

In large secondary schools, senior management teams (in the best circumstances) supply policies and procedures which are communicated to staff swiftly and efficiently. Such action results in a common ethos and effectiveness. Of course, open discussion of such policies and procedures is vital. But a head's influence and character are of crucial importance in the successful implementation of policies. Nevertheless, despite the weight of administrative responsibility his or her door should be open to the most junior of staff. Lack of consultation and openness leads to a bad atmosphere in the staff room and affects work throughout the school.

Despite heavy responsibiltiies, the best heads still manage to teach. In small primary schools the head necessarily teaches most of the time and comes to know each and every child and their families intimately. In larger primary schools and in secondary schools the amount a head can teach is, of course, variable, but to be seen to teach is important to staff and pupils. Many heads of quite large schools know many of their pupils and the communities the school serves – all powerful forces for the good.

Some of the best heads I have met were the poorest administrators and vice versa. With the emphasis on 'management' now fashionable, it is to be hoped that traditional qualities are not relegated or delegated.

The teacher at the primary school is largely a general class teacher and not a specialist. Those who have specialist knowledge or flair, as artists, musicians, naturalists or whatever, are of great value for they are likely to light fires of interest in the children as well as sharing their expertise with other teachers.

At the secondary stage subject-mindedness is crucial at all levels of the ability range. What is known and loved is communicated with enthusiasm and delight. Basic to all this is generosity and open-mindedness. From such teachers at all levels something rubs off – even on the most disaffected pupil. Think of the opposite effect at this critical time. A teacher whose heart is not in the job and who is idle and narrow in outlook will waste the time when the mind is most receptive.

Relationships

Good relationships in a school have a magical, elusive quality recognised but not easy to pin down. Like all seemingly effortless matters, behind them lies a mass of planning and skill followed by hard decisions. Decisions involve risk and sometimes disappointment: uniform, school expeditions, links with parents, school records, time allocation for subjects etc., etc., are all important matters to clarify.

The best schools have a simple organisation and a few rules which have been hard fought. Curriculum, buildings, organisation of classes, pastoral care arrangements all influence relationships. Some secondary schools are now top-heavy with staff concerned with 'caring', but the class teacher or form tutor is the key person and needs time to get to know individuals, collect opinions about progress and achievement and see to it that what is known is *used* to benefit a pupil's work and self-esteem. Too many pupils receive less informative than they should about their progress and about what they should do to improve their work.

In the last analysis the vast majority of schools, along with parents, attempt to civilise their charges by example, by fostering the ideals of public service, by concern for the individual and through the curriculum. It is an uphill job but, judging from the great majority of human behaviour, surprisingly successful. In all schools, from inner-city to leading public school and from nursery school to sixth form, the unwritten code is that order is better than chaos, knowledge than ignorance, gentleness than violence, courtesy than rudeness.

A broad and balanced curriculum

Children have a right to a solid, broad general education and not to be bored. Indeed, one of the most noticeable features of a 'caring' school is not a plethora of pastoral staff but a good curriculum well taught. Such a curriculum gives the basis for a good life whether in good times or bad times. Breadth, balance and coherence are the essentials of a good curriculum at all levels of ability. The first two are obvious in meaning. The need (for example) to find ways of providing a broad coarse in science at secondary level which includes elements from the three main branches of science – physics, chemistry and biology – yet one that leaves time for a range of other subjects so that the curriculum for an individual is broad and balanced. The National Curriculum is working towards this end. Within a few years it will become simpler and its testing will be equally transformed; it is important that testing should not bite too hard into precious teaching time and distort the content and methods of teaching.

Coherence means a curriculum bound together by the threads of mathematics, science and language. Will a pupil link a lesson on crop production in geography with a knowledge of plant growth learned in science? To achieve this, links between science, technology and geography are necessary. Do English teachers capitalise in their lessons on what has been done in science to give strength to written work in English and so on? Coherence is not easy to achieve because subject departments tend to work in relative isolation, but to do so gives pupils some glimpses of the wholeness of knowledge.

In the earlier years of the primary school right until the top juniors, or even beyond to 12 or 13, the subdivisions of learning and knowledge into 'subjects' is of little significance to the children. Language and mathematics pervade most subjects as do the arts. Nevertheless, even at this stage mathematics and English still require systematic study in their own right.

For most pupils in a secondary school up to the age of 16 the same *subjects* should be taught but with different treatments according to ability. If our primary need is for skilled people with high ideals and personal standards, vocational courses for some (the less academic) which emphasise the three Rs and a little manual dexterity will not do. Courses for these boys and girls need to involve just as hard a struggle for them *intellectually* as those designed for the more academic.

135

Up to 16 the basis of a common culture should be established. The great unifying concepts of science – energy, the structure of matter, evolution, the balance of nature – should be taught to those who have any chance of grasping them, however fleetingly. The big ideas of other subjects need similar attention. And for whatever ability, the significance of what they are taught should be the touchstone. In this regard, personal, social and moral implications should be considered when they arise in traditional subjects or at their interface. As stressed a moment ago, much closer co-operation between subjects is necessary at certain points to develop this.

With regard to ethnic minorities, respect for and knowledge of their cultures are important. Work in the normal subjects of the curriculum can be, and often is, enriched by opportunities to study the ethnic and cultural variety of modern life by pupils contributing from their own experience so that pupils are made aware of both the commonality and diversity of differing cultures. It is self-evident that work on the beliefs, values and culture of the home of ethnic minorities or children from the majority community needs to be handled sensitively. Misunderstandings can take place; for example, if certain patterns of behaviour are wrongly assumed to be common to all: alcohol use, sexual relationships, and nutrition and eating habits are some examples of sensitive issues.

Time taken on special courses (e.g. 'Black Studies') is misplaced. While respect for their beliefs, values and culture is essential, most families and children want to be taught basic subjects that will help them to progress here in the West. To them mathematics, science, technology, English, and so on are vital to progress.

Good teaching and a good curriculum is the key to good behaviour. Children who 'look up and are not fed' lose respect, become troublesome and are likely to play truant.

Organisational devices which give a pupil a level of work which suits him

None can be discussed coolly. The correct scientific principle to apply to organisation is that each one of us is unique genetically and needs a unique environment to maximise potential.

It follows form this that it is *just* to treat different people differently so long as each is treated as well as possible. On this argument mixed-ability teaching is the right approach, since each pupil will have a different treatment – that is, a different environment in order to bring out the best in him or her. Streaming is a coarse instrument and simply groups children together on a single criterion such as IQ or ability at mathematics. It allows (in the best circumstances) children to go at their own pace without either being held back by the slow or discouraged by the superiority of the fast.

Faced with practical problems schools quite rightly compromise between individual attention in a class and grouping, streaming and setting children of roughly similar abilities. Most primary schools are now unstreamed, but in each class ability groups are often formed for different activities. In small village schools where age and ability is mixed, slow children learn from the quick, who in turn learn from helping the slow.

Middle and secondary schools vary but use both 'banding' (coarse streaming) to group pupils and mixed-ability arrangements. In both, setting is used to group similar abilities in subjects like mathematics.

For most secondary schools and their teachers mixed-ability arrangements do not fulfil the basic principle stated earlier. Mixed-ability groups are generally taught by whole-class methods and, for example, brighter children remain unchallenged by work pitched at or around the class norm. In addition, in a mixed-ability organisation teachers spend much time on lesson preparation and too little on marking and class discussion. These deficiencies impede diagnosis of disability or of high ability and prevent suitable levels of work being set.

Observations suggest that banding and setting policies help most teachers to sustain the right *general* level of demand and stimulus, but pupils here seldom get individual attention – and there is always the danger of some pupils being misplaced and labelled so that teacher expectation, which is very important, operates in the wrong direction.

Organisation is important for helping a child to develop his potential but it is of much less importance than the quality of the teacher and the influence of the head.

Awareness of moral values

At first, rules need to be imposed by home and school as referred to in the last chapter, and some need to persist: to be honest, truthful and to abhor cruelty in any form. As children grow up they come to understand the basis of restraints of one kind or another at home and school and accept them. In this way they gradually learn a measure of tolerance, to make allowances, and to share, to find out where they stand with family and friends and what they can expect of them and what family and friends can ask of them. In the development of these attitudes most schools, from early on, teach children to respect their surroundings and take care of books and other materials and equipment. Co-operative work provides abundant opportunities for teaching how and why to behave in a responsible and considerate way. And, very important, both home and school will teach about choice between doing or saying this or that. The ability to choose between alternatives requires the ability to reason, a capacity which lies at the heart of morality, the ability to think through the consequence of one's actions or words.

Morality is best learned through example at home and school. Teachers who themselves are fair, turn up on time at lessons, do their marking well, do not make idle threats, prepare their work, occasionally 'explode', and so on, are good exemplars.

In discussion at the secondary stage a teacher must be prepared to show tolerance for the extreme opinion. The need for tolerance should never be taken as indifference, which may give the impression that one answer is as good as another and that no conviction is worth holding passionately. Tolerance towards the opinions of the young, however crudely and violently they are expressed, should combine with clear convictions of lasting importance in the teacher himself.

Critical times and the lottery of family and school

I indicated earlier that only the vaguest idea of the timing and extent of critical times exists for ourselves. I have identified a number of key periods of importance between conception and puberty. It is not possible to say whether any one critical period is more influential than another. Children are resilient and after a bad start may catch up. The tragedy is a train of adverse circumstances: poor home followed by poor schools. This combination is a disaster and happens to many children now.

For many children school is their only hope of bettering themselves, and of escape. Most schools are a source of stimulus and sound learning, but some two million pupils out of six million experience poor teaching.[2] Inner-city pupils are much more likely to suffer from poor and shoddy teaching than others. They need sympathy (but not sentimentality) for their conditions of life. Much more important is good teaching and high expectations.

Many of the adverse circumstances I have outlined in Chapter 12 impinge on the inner-city child, though one should never forget rural deprivation, which is ever-present but spread out thinly.

Two facts dealt with in this book are important for provision and for choice of school: the staggering rate of growth of the brain and intellect up to 5, which continues at a slower pace through the primary years; and the uniqueness of the individual child.

With regard to the first fact, during the pre-school years a child acquires skills, expectancies and notions about the world and about people at enormous pace.[3] Yet some of the very best pre-school provision, state nursery schools and classes, is in short supply in England, as Chapter 6 makes clear. There is good evidence that pre-school education can improve the quality of life of young children and their families. Specifically it will enhance a child's cognitive development and thus improve his or her educational potential and, in the long term, overall performance.[4]

The actual type of pre-school education seems to matter little on the evidence, provided the child receives proper care, has interesting activities and other children to play with. Investment in it, and the improved quality of life it brings, is likely to pay good dividends throughout the primary school and perhaps well beyond.[4]

Of course, pre-school education can only provide a basis for future progress in schools and homes that will build on pre-school work. The worrying point here is *lack* of good provision. For most children state nursery provision, which is the ideal, does not exist.

The Introduction to this book argued for more money to be directed away from military expenditure to education and health. The average annual cost in 1988/89 of a nursery and primary school place was £1,102, a secondary 11–16 place £1,594, and a sixth-form place £2,551.[5] Assuming seven years of nursery and primary education plus five years of secondary education, the total unit cost of schooling for a leaver at 16 would be £15,684. Think of what the cost of the Gulf War would have bought in improved quality of education! This is said with no disrespect for the bravery of our armed forces. Besides improved provision there is a further financial point: that the growth of the intellect during the nursery and primary years warrants a marked improvement in the unit costs for schools in these particularly crucial years of development. At present their annual cost is less than half that of a sixth-form place but the pace of intellectual development is much faster in the earlier than the later years and the pay-off, as mentioned, could be impressive.

With regard to the second fact, to crush individuality in any circumstances is the road to general mediocrity but diversity *between* schools is not essential to foster individual potential. Well-resourced, co-educational comprehensive schools with a broad curriculum and the flexible organisational policies described earlier in this chapter are sufficient to provide the right environment for most children up to the statutory school-leaving age, but single-sex secondary schools should be on offer for parents to take up or reject where possible.

Despite government policy on the importance of choice of school, many parents will in practice have little choice, their child going to the nearest school; this is why I have argued that *all* schools should be made better. And it is the case that some schools and some teachers remain obstinately better than others – like families. Luck in the family and luck with teachers are, with health, the greatest blessings a child can have. Policy-makers, school governors and heads can do only so much towards achieving good schools. Quality of teachers must be their first priority, that is, teachers who can inspire. What to teach, how, where and what with, are of lesser importance.

Underlying these practical matters are two biological principles: the notion of critical times in the growth and development of the brain and the fact of inherited differences which make each one of us unique. Both should make for unease about shoddy teaching, gaps in provision, the failure to recognise that equality of opportunity implies diversity of treatment, league tables of schools based on examination results and sink schools. The two principles should constantly remind us that all children need protection from political ideology and ignorant parents.

References

1 DES, *Special Educational Needs* (HMSO, 1978).
2 DES, *Standards in Education, 1988–89* (HMSO, 1990).
3 J. S. Bruner, 'Poverty and childhood', *Oxford Review of Education* 1 (1975).
4 A. F. Osborn and J. E. Milbank, *The Effects of Early Education* (Oxford University Press, 1987).
5 Chartered Institute of Public Finance and Accountancy, *Handbook of Education Unit Costs, 1988/89* (CIPFA, 1990).

INDEX

142